THE MENTOR MODEL

Tools to Building and Sustaining a Healthy Mentor-

Mentee Relationship Long-term

Felicia M. Fort

The Mentor Model

Cover design by LB Graphic Design

ISBN 978-1-5468-0199-3 (trade paperback)

Published by Felicia Fort
www.onestepcloser2.com
ffort@onestepcloser2.com

Printed in the United States of America

ACKNOWLEDGMENTS

I would like to give special thanks to the mentors and mentees that helped in shaping my life and inspired me to give my whole self to them. I have been blessed to travel down the road of mentorship, and each of you have impacted my personal and professional life in many different ways. I would not be where I am today without influence. You all have significantly impacted my life and contributed to my success and level of maturity, and for that I thank you. Sheila Savar, Lucretia Glover, Shervon Yancey, and Solomon Hill were my mentors from the very beginning. Although you came into my life at different times, I gained valuable lessons from your leadership and your experience. To my bosses (former and current) throughout my journey of professional development and maturity, I want to say thank you for pouring into me what leadership is and making an investment in my growth, knowledge and skillset within your organizations. My mentees: Aaron M. Williams and Jideka Long, the love I have for you both is unexplainable. Knowing you both since you were 12 years of age and seeing you blossom and sprout into your own unique selves that the world is waiting to discover—future leaders. To my eldest mentee, Aye Diallo, the day I spoke at your intern orientation was the day you boldly asked for me to be your mentor. From that moment, I could tell that you were a leader by birth. You boldly took a step toward your vision and went after everything you said you wanted to achieve. I learned so much from you, and I thank you for asking me to be your mentor and not accepting anything less. To my rock, Fatima Fort—my oldest sister and other half, you have challenged me to be the person I thought I could never become. Even when you didn't know you were inspiring me, you were. With your solid expressions of how you show love, you have always been there for me, and I will always be there for you. To Fantasia, Fayvia, and Francine—my social butterfly sisters—I do this because of you—to inspire and motivate you all to push through and to live an extraordinary life with God. We had it rough, but so have diamonds and other fine pieces of jewels. We are meant to succeed and build our collective empire. We are destined to have everything that we ever said we wanted in life. You all are true "Go-Getters" and I learn from each of you daily. To my parents, Janice Fort and Barry Bryant, thank you for your survival and never giving up on me. You both hold a special place in my heart. This book is about what a mentor is, but you have pulled me away from the strongholds that you each simultaneously fought through for years and you allowed me to discover on my own the difference between wrong and right and allowed me follow my own path, so I thank you. To my nephew, Jamir Lewis and my two nieces, Jumeriah and Ashlee White, I want you to have something to be inspired through our family legacy and our generational blessing. You can do all things through Christ. To all my family members, I love you all and thank you for your support and fist pumps.

To all the mentor organizations that I have been a part of: the YWCA (EMPOwERgirlz Mentoring Program), Benedict College (Leadership Institute and Mentoring Program), Black Male CUNY Initiative Program, FosterCare 2 Success (OFA Program), Imentor Program of New York, and Best Kids. I would not have been as effective and open to the importance of having mentee's and becoming a dedicated mentor without your programs, trainings, and leadership, so with that I thank you all. To my Nonprofit, One Step Closer Foundation, I thank you for never allowing me to slow down, but always giving my clients and partners 150% of my efforts. You have allowed me to imprint our motto *Mentorship through Mathematics*. Allowing me to continuously inspire individuals of all ages, backgrounds, and experience levels, by instilling in each one the support, guidance, and commitment to understanding mathematics. We never gave up on anyone and provided services through the Summer Externship Program (SEP), College Care Package Program, Tutoring Program, Fort's Book Scholarship Program, and the College Tour Program. We have managed to stay connected to all of our clients that have come through our program. To my apprentices, thank you for allowing me to play your surrogate mentor, thank you for making the SEP Program a success. To Ayden M. Williams, a client, future apprentice and friend, you have inspired me to be a better communicator with youth under the age of 13 years old and you taught me to value everyone's feedback and opinions regardless of age. I would like to give thanks to my co-mentors that have poured their mentorship experiences into this book: Krystal Leaphart, Sankaya Hall, Solomon Hill, Linnita Holsten, Fayvia Cromartie-White, Elizabeth Strong, Lucretia Glover, Twanisha Johnson, Aaron M. Williams, and Jideka Long. You all have inspired me to continue to pour into my mentees as I watched each of you do the same. Together we are strengthening our next generation by instilling in them what our mentors instilled in us.

TABLE OF CONTENTS

This piece of literature is written as a guide for those seeking mentorship—either as a mentor or as a mentee. The goal of this book is to offer insight on how to establish a healthy, productive, and mutually-beneficial relationship through mentoring. Mentoring is a relationship between a mentor (professional, role model) and a mentee (the learner, one who is in the developmental phase, whether it be through academic development, professional development, personal development, mental development, spiritual development, or more). This book was written for you to read in its entirety as it provides a wealth of information that is critical to all parties that make up the mentoring relationship. However, this book is also useful for those looking to identify timely and concrete solutions to the mentoring experience; whether one is seeking to become a mentee, a parent is looking for guidance on understanding the mentoring relationship, or if a mentor is looking for ways to improve their relationship with their mentee. This book includes real-life scenarios, self-development activities, and practical ideas and tools for the mentorship experience.

The Mentor Model was written through the lens of first-hand experience, evidence-based research, and real-life dos and don'ts of the contributing authors that sought to find or sustain a relationship with a mentor or a mentee. It has been proven through many successful people such as, Oprah Winfrey that every person who has reached a level of success has had the help of a mentor. In several interviews that featured Ms. Winfrey, when a question is posed that deals with role models, mentors or people who inspires, she always acknowledges Barbara Walters and Mya Angelou as those people that fill that role. The goal of this book is to inspire and educate young and experienced professionals to seek after mentees, and for adolescents, teenage youth, and young adults to seek after a mentor. The mentoring experience provides the mentee and the mentor a mutual beneficial relationship, meaning that the outcome is portioned equally; whatever the mentor gives, the mentee has to give as well. The relationship will only work when both recipients are putting in the effort. Although there are many benefits to mentoring, there are also challenging phases throughout the experience. The reason why they are referred to as phases is because they too shall pass. According to Dictionary.com, a phase is "a stage in a process of change or development," through the mentorship process, especially when dealing with humans, many of us go through change or development. When mentoring a youth, they go through changes whether it is transitioning from middle school, to high school, to college or puberty. As a mentor, we tend to change through statuses: career, relationship, parental, or just more responsibilities to manage. This book touches on those benefits and challenges, and answers daunting questions such as, "Is this the right fit?" This book will also guide the mentor through scenarios on how to handle difficult situations that many mentors experience, to equip you better to handle them when they arise. Mentoring is a commitment and an ongoing learning experience through the phases of the relationship. At every stage of the process, you will learn something new about the mentee and yourself (the mentor). There is always something that benefits you whether you're the mentee or the mentor. This book will provide clarity for questions such as: We do not have anything in common? Is mentoring intended to be a lifetime relationship? One might ask, "How many mentors should a mentee have?" Or, "How many mentees can a mentor have?" The answers are in this book.

Mentoring is a part of life, whether you know it or not. It's everywhere; it's affiliated with many companies, schools, and extracurricular activities. Whether many call it a mentor, a role model or an individual leader – the act of mentorship is being demonstrated. In today's modern companies, many of them set up workplace mentoring also known as "informal mentoring relationship," which is a learning partnership between seasoned "old hands" employees and novices "entry level" employees to help beginners learn the ropes. This is considered an informal workplace relationship because this relationship was not built on commonality, but the pairing process was based on a generic match only to meet specific agency objectives or complete a project and not with someone who you eventually want to learn their position. Formal mentoring relationships allow organizations to create relationships by matching more experienced employees (mentors) with less experienced employees (mentees) to help those individuals in the mentoring relationship to identify and develop their own talents and possibly assist them to elevate to the next position. This is considered an investment because someone is willing to assist another with their personal and professional development for free. Mentorship is a free opportunity to invest in, if they had stocks or bonds for this benefit, we would all jump on it. It is a high commodity that many people are looking into as an adult. Many adults are looking back questioning why they didn't consider getting a mentor when they were younger, but the best thing about mentorship is that there is no age limit. Now in accounting, it's always better when one receives an ROI (return on investment), and mentoring defiantly tends to pay off well when a mentor commits to putting in the work to make a mentoring relationship thrive with a mentee and vice versa.

The return is the results (growth) and the outcome of that person that was made from time commitments. Research shows that through the mentorship relationship, mentees advance more quickly, earn higher salaries, and gain more satisfaction in their jobs and lives than their peers who do not have mentors. Remember, this relationship is mutually effective; mentors tend to live more abundantly when they know they have helped change another person's outcome and they receive more than they desire. For employers who have implemented workplace mentoring in their companies, the benefits are higher performance and greater success in attracting, developing, and retaining talent. In companies, high executives such as, CEOs have mentors too; they just refer to them as coaches. This book outlines the different alias for the word "mentor" and "mentee" that many may reference.

The Mentor Model is just that; a guide that leads a mentor or a potential mentor through the: who, what, when, where, why, and how questions of getting to a sustainable, lasting relationship with their mentee. This book offers personal testimonies and experiences from a range of individuals who can identify with the benefits of being a mentor and a mentee. These individuals experienced different benefits from this connection and provided the ins and outs of their role as the mentor or the mentee. You will also notice that many of the contributing models have experienced both sides of the field and brings a different perspective based on where they were at that time in their lives. They reveal the benefits and challenges with being a mentor and how to deal with a "perfect" youth and to a youth who does not have all the necessities to succeed. What is it that every youth needs to prepare them for success? What is it that every mentor needs to make sure they are giving as well as receiving? I believe that every reader whether a youth, adolescent, young professional, middle aged professional, high executive, or parent would benefit from this book. One should read it with one goal in mind: "Success begets success." Everyone needs a model, someone to lead them along the way. Oliver Goldsmith said it best, "people seldom improve when they have no other model but themselves to copy." This book will motivate, teach, and help one uncover their truest potential and overcome hardships and build relationships for the betterment of people. This book will give you a different perspective and create new ideas for your mentor-mentee relationship (new or matured). Why not lift as we climb? The more mentors that we have willing to change a life for the better, the better our future generation will become.

THE DEMAND

Similar to an entrepreneur's objective, when starting a business in a particular market or industry a demand analysis is taken, which surveys whether the need for something is high and whether the type of consumers will benefit from this and refer another. The demand analysis helps find out the optimum quantity of goods and services to be produced so that different quantities can be supplied[1]. Well, this worked in Big Brothers Big Sisters Program. The demand is high (many saw the benefit of being a mentee and referred others). However, the supply is low. Yes, the need for mentors to match these mentees are low. "More than 34,000 children across the United States, primarily boys of color, are on Big Brothers Big Sisters "waiting to be matched lists." [2] Comparing this sample to the whole United States youth population, under 18 years old, approximately 7 million of these youth are considered "at risk," which means prisons are being made and new statistics are being documented just for them. To prevent these pipeline to prison statistics, more mentors are needed. Mentoring is a way to place a dent in

---

[1] http://www.wisenepali.com/2015/01/importance-of-demand-analysis-in.html
[2] Big Brothers Big Sisters https://e8k0luq9wg.execute-api.us-east
1.amazonaws.com/v1/articles/9550433/big_brother_big_sisters_of_ame.amp

these numbers by providing guidance and fostering support for these vulnerable young people. Mentoring is open to everyone, and organizations that support matching and making connections rely on volunteers to help sustain the program. Like many businesses, the success and failure relies in the hands of the consumers (volunteers). Without consumers for a business, its unsustainable, the same goes for mentorship relationships, without mentors for sufficient long-term mentoring matches, then the organization will fail to supply the need. Mentors play pivotal roles in young peoples' lives by offering a compassionate ear or actively teaching and inspiring curiosity. With the supply being so high for mentors, the demand for many of the youth (mentees) who are waiting to be placed with a mentor have experienced the following in their lifetime are high as well:

- Homeless youth.
- Youth in foster care.
- Youth with disabilities.
- Youth involved in delinquent activities.
- Youth who have an incarcerated parent or been in the juvenile system.
- Pregnant youth or teen parents.

Knowing that there is a high percentage of youth from special populations and complicated backgrounds is contrary to who will actually take a youth on. After reading an article from Youth.Gov, resulted a survey that quantified how many adults were willing to mentor a youth from a complicated background, out of 100 adults, 100% were willing too; however, when it was the actual time to mentor them, the number reporting back was not as high.[3]

Many children in underserved communities are unaware and are not privileged to these resources or organizations that offer these benefits. We need more mentors to change the lives of the next generation. The survey suggested that the largest areas of need are for youth involved in the juvenile justice system as well as those who are pregnant or teen parents. While research suggests that there are challenges and risks associated with working with at-risk youth, it has also found substantial benefits for these populations. For example, studies have found benefits for youth involved in foster care, youth with an incarcerated parent(s), and youth who have been involved in delinquent behavior.[4]

---

[3] Youth.gov. http://youth.gov/youth-topics/mentoring/types-mentoring-relationships#sthash.1cwRLil0.dpuf

[4] Youth.gov. http://youth.gov/youth-topics/mentoring/types-mentoring-relationships#sthash.1cwRLil0.dpuf

If I was not introduced to someone outside of my immediate environment, I probably would have been a statistic. I am a former foster youth raised through the foster care system from 7- 21 years of age, due to an unhealthy home environment infested with drugs, abandonment and violence. Changing environments was the best thing that ever happened to me because I was exposed to different opportunities and people. My mindset was broadened and I was enlightened to things outside of my box called "The hood." It wasn't until I was seventeen years old that I realized that people were rooting for me to succeed—social workers, teachers, bosses, extended family members, and peers. Graduating from high school with high honors and getting accepted into college changed my life for the better. In that moment, I realized that the stigma of being pregnant, homeless, a drug user, or dead, was not my destiny. I was surrounded by surrogate mentors, not "official" mentors, but people who supported my decisions and guided me through them. Sometimes as young adults, we have been surrogate mentors, by just assisting youth in our neighborhoods, encouraging youth to finish school, or that child we use to babysit for extra money, we just wanted the best for that individual. My official mentoring relationship began my sophomore year of college with a woman named Ms. Lucretia

Glover. As a full time staff member at Benedict College, Ms. Glover worked in the School of Science, Technology, Engineering, and Mathematics (STEM), she held a Bachelor of Science degree from Benedict College in Math Education and a Masters from Cambridge University. As a result of me being a math major, I was in a position that I didn't really know what I wanted to pursue with my degree once I finished. After getting acquainted with Ms. Glover and knowing that her background was mathematics, I asked if she could mentor me because I wanted someone to guide my decisions and assist me with them as well.

After understanding the benefits of having a mentor, I started accepting mentors for every aspect of my vision. For example, Ms. Glover mentored me in math. After that, I needed mentors that understood entrepreneurship, spirituality, mentors who were authors, and political business leaders. Now I didn't find all of my aspirations in one person, so I was able to find them in multiple people and build my mentorship relationship by having multiple mentors. Before anyone can see that mentorship relationship, you have to first know where you fall. Are you a mentor looking for a mentee or a mentee looking for a mentor?

18

Mentor Pre-Qualification Checklist

- Are you available?

- Do you want to share your knowledge and experience with others?

- Are you a good listener?

- Do you enjoy encouraging and motivating others?

- Are you comfortable asking challenging questions?

- Do you want to contribute to other people's growth and success?

- Are you comfortable with someone depending on your expertise?

- Are you prepared to invest your time in mentoring on a regular basis?

- Are you adaptable?

- Do you know how to inspire another person?

PART I:

THE ROLE OF

A MENTOR

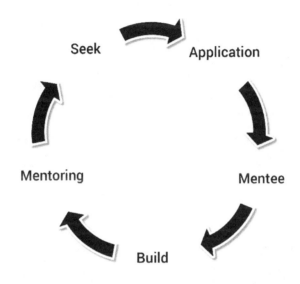

"A mentor is someone who allows you to see the hope inside yourself."

~**Oprah Winfrey**

A proclamation is a formal public and official announcement of an important matter. Any elected official can present a proclamation, but many are most familiar with proclamations that are issued by mayors and presidents. There are two types of proclamations issued by the United States President: "ceremonial," which designate special observances or celebrate national holidays, and "substantive," which usually relates to the conduct of foreign affairs and other sworn executive duties. [5]

It has been nationally recognized that the entire month of January of every year will be National "I am A Mentor Day." This is one of the benefits of being a mentor. We have a national recognition of all the relationships that have been built and sustained throughout the years. On multiple social media platforms, you will see pictures of the bonding relationships or the results of what a mentor has done for that mentee. There will also be recruitment post about getting involved in mentoring from different organizations who need mentors. It was inaugurated in 2002, but during Barack Obama's presidential years, he made a commitment to continue to honor the month by doing a ceremonial proclamation every year. Our 44th President Barack Obama, highlighted the importance of what a mentor can do and the

---

[5] https://en.wikipedia.org/wiki/Presidential_proclamation

impact it leaves on our future generation. Along these lines, President Obama created the My Brother's Keeper Initiative, which is also a call to action for Americans to help make a difference in the lives of young people by becoming mentors. My Brother's Keeper Initiative has shown positive outcomes and therefore is a centerpiece of mentoring. This initiative promotes and emphasizes the effects mentoring has on every individual and the success rates these programs have for participating young people. My Brother's Keeper Initiative reminds us that mentors matter and having a mentor-mentee relationship is invaluable.

Mentoring is not a second job or a burden that can negatively impact your schedule or take control of your individuality. It is a lending of one's time, knowledge, and influence that can fundamentally change the life of another person. President Obama and others that heed the call, cannot do this by themselves, the belief is that we all do better when everyone has a fair shot at reaching for their dreams. Maya Angelou said it best, "In order to be a mentor, and an effective one, one must care. You must care."

Behind every successful person, there's a mentor who helped them along the way, whether they were there from the beginning or at a pivotal part in their life. Here is a list of mentor-mentee relationships that you may be familiar with:

MENTOR	MENTEE	Quotes by the mentee
Maya Angelou	Oprah Winfrey	"Mentors are important and I don't think anybody makes it in the world without some form of mentorship."
Benjamin E. Mays	Dr. Martin Luther King Jr.	"Good protégés have several different mentors, and learn different things from each of them. The best mentors are happy to see their protégés become more famous than they are, and don't try to hold them back."
Larry Summer	Sheryl Sandberg	"Mentors and sponsors are crucial to success. But the relationships should develop more naturally and be more reciprocal than anything else."

Wiley Pittman	Ray Charles	"He took the time to teach me music. Somehow he knew in his heart, this kid loves music so much, I'm going to do whatever I can to help him learn how to play."
Sir Freddie Laker	Richard Branson	"It's always good to have a helping hand at the start."
Multiple mentors	Indra Nooyi	"If I hadn't had mentors, I wouldn't be here today. I am a product of great mentoring."
Luther Powell	Collin Powell	"All of us have the ability to serve as a mentor."

CHAPTER 1: What is a Mentor?

By sharing their own stories and offering guidance and advice, mentors can instill a sense of infinite possibility in the hearts and minds of their mentees, demonstrating that with hard work and passion, nothing is beyond their potential. One of the first records in literature the word "mentor" was found in Homer's *The Odyssey*. In the story, a wise man was given the name "Mentor" his task was to assist and educate Odysseus' son, Telemachus. In the story Odysseus went to fight in the Trojan War, **he entrusted the care of his** kingdom and his **son to Mentor**, who was known as a **wise and trusted counselor**.[6] A mentor is an individual, usually older, or more experienced, who helps guide another individual's development. Every young person and parent can benefit from having a "mentor."

Mentors come in all shapes, sizes, and experience. If you close your eyes and think about all the people who have impacted your life, you will defiantly come up with your own personal definition of the word. Some mentors played a central role in your development, the decisions you made, and

---

[6] The Journal of Extension (JOE). http://www.joe.org/joe/2010december/tt8.php

the paths you chose to take, others influenced you even without your awareness. When you tie everything together, the mentor's ultimate role is to guide, to give advice, motivate, push by encouraging, advocate, teach, and to support the mentee. A mentor can help a person (mentee) improve his or her abilities and skills through observation, assessment, modeling, and by providing guidance which at the end has a profound effect on the mentee.

Mentoring typically happens during three periods of a person's life that are categorized as: youth mentoring, academic mentoring, and workplace mentoring. There are distinctions among the three. Youth mentoring involves a relationship that evolves through personal, emotional, cognitive, and psychological growth between an adolescent and a young or seasoned adult. Academic mentoring typifies the "apprentice model of education" [7]where a faculty member imparts knowledge, provides support, and offers guidance to a student mentee on academic as well as non-academic (e.g. personal problems, identity crises) issues. My experience of academic mentoring as an undergraduate in college with Ms. Glover, was making sure that my program of study aligned to what I eventually wanted to do after I graduated. Her

---

[7] www.ncbi.nlm.nih.gov

guidance and shared experience taught me what not to do and what to proceed in doing. Finally, workplace mentoring occurs in an organizational setting and the purpose is the personal and professional growth of the mentee. The mentor may be a supervisor, someone else within the organization but outside the mentee's chain of command, or an individual in another organization. The longevity of the mentoring relationship has proven to be a key component in both the development of the mentoring relationship and in the resulting outcomes. It takes time for a young person to trust a mentor, and in many ways, the relationship doesn't even begin until trust is formed. Long-lasting relationships with clearly defined roles will increase the likelihood of positive youth outcomes.

As mentioned earlier, mentoring can be formed through formal or informal relationships. However, majority of the mentoring relationships formed between youth and adults are through informal relationships which started just through a conversation or mutual contact. Maybe a parent asking a young adult leader in the community to mentor their youth. These adults do not receive training or support from a structured organization or program nor sign a contract to abide by when dealing with youth. It has been reported that only 29 percent of mentored relationships are formal, which means they went through a structured process. This number may seem low, but in all reality when going through a formal process many organizations are only mandating that you stay committed to your mentee and the program for at most two years. However, the ultimate goal is that you stay committed to your mentee relationship outside of the program, which then turns into an informal mentoring relationship. Therefore, the number is low because of the organizations relationship commitment terms. Within formal mentoring programs, the structure of the program can also differ per organization. On the other hand some mentoring programs provide clear goals with training and support while others are more flexible, with loose goals and limited training and support.

Mentor Alias

A mentor comes with different experiences, levels of education, employment history, functionalities, and names ("Titles"). Mending mentoring relationships involves a whole host of mentor styles that one has to understand and monitor. Mentoring has been used in many different ways, many people don't necessarily use the term "mentor" to describe their relationships.

The Coach. The Coach is someone who through executive title, seniority, or status within an organization or community has reached the pinnacle of his or her career and is worthy of and willing to impart knowledge and wisdom into another person, community or organization. Often known as experienced leaders, they have learned by building relationships and having mentors throughout their lifetime. Coaches are sometimes free, but when it is business related, they tend to offer a service fee to get you where you need to go. This is advised for individuals who are more established and/or have a vision and need some direction in a particular field (i.e. Business).

The Sponsor. This person is intentional about opening doors for their mentee, referring the mentee to others, and promoting the mentee's talents.

The Teacher. The Teacher could be an educator, working with current or past students to build their professional talents and skills, or someone who assumes the "honorary" role of teacher—promoting learning and growth by imparting knowledge, debating ideas, or recommending resources.

The Peer Mentor. Peer Mentors "accountability partner" a person who is along the same age helps the other person keep a commitment. Colleagues or friends pair up to help each other grow within an organization. They might team up to gain professional development experience, share networking contacts, or simply support each other's career path choices.

The Friend. This person accepts the mentee for who they are and engages in a more personal relationship that supports the mentee in their personal and professional growth.

The Self-Help Mentor. The Self-Help Mentor takes the form of books, vision boards, manuals, articles, checklists, software, websites, and so forth that provide proven formulas or step-by-step advice on how to grow professionally. While not a substitute for an actual person, some of these popular resources are useful in helping individuals map out transitions through schooling, a specific career path or lay a foundation for future mentoring relationships.

The Inner Mentor. The Inner Mentor is the internal voice that calls upon intuition to glean and mold life experiences into a personalized leadership philosophy. This nontraditional self-mentoring approach takes into account past experiences, current competencies, and future possibilities. The process of mentoring yourself is difficult—it takes concentration, self-reflection, and the ability to trust your own instincts.

The Self-Evaluation Process

Many people believe that the steps to becoming a mentor is simply to find a mentee that is looking for a mentor. That is completely wrong. The first step is self-evaluation. Are you ready to guide a person younger or less experienced than you and provide an avenue for them to come to you as a reliable and trustworthy source? Think about it, a mentor is someone who provides resources, time, insight, transparency, a wealth of information, and engaging experiences to better the life of their mentee. Mentors though are not always right—they are humans with flaws like everyone else.

Mentors do not exist to take the place of the parent or fill in the spot of a babysitter. Mentors that work with youth, work alongside the parent to make the overall experience and youth development process less stressful by helping youth to avoid major problems and make positive decisions on their own. Mentors are not there to watch the youth (mentee) while the parent is attending a girls or guys night out. Many people that volunteer to become mentors have a misconception that mentoring only entails providing advice. According to those in the field, "You are part counselor, coach, friend, sponsor, master, teacher, and therapist, all rolled into one. An effective mentor can seamlessly transition from one role to another based on a mentee's needs at the time".[8]

It is paramount that as a mentor, you take time out to ask yourself whether or not you are able to fully commit to your mentee. Communication is a key quality to knowing if the mentor role is for you. Being transparent with your feelings and thoughts is the best way to transmit acceptance and maintain an authentic relationship. The weight of availability, which is how much your mentee expects you to be available, varies depending on the age of your mentee. The younger your mentee, the more available you should be, especially if they are in there teens, the need to feel embraced and heard is important. Some mentor relationships last a few weeks, while others last years. Some of this depends on whether the mentee is confident that you can play the proper role for them. This all boils down to, are you available when they need you?

Self-evaluation is the answer to everything that deals with you and owning up to this role. When evaluating, remember that mentees pick up good habits as well as bad habits. When you self-evaluate, you become an active

---

[8] Vincent O'Connell - http://www.fastcompany.com/3043553/work-smart/5-steps-to-becoming-an-amazing-mentor

participant in your own assessment. Your involvement enables you to honestly assess your strengths and also areas you need to improve. Through this process, authenticity and transparency are key to help determine if you are responsible in certain areas of your life because you do not want to instill bad habits onto your mentee who is looking for guidance. Are you a responsible person? Do you set goals and achieve them? Can you give someone good and reliable advice? Can someone depend on your conversation and trust you? Are you a good friend to others? Do you believe in higher education? These questions can help determine if you are ready to commit. Be clear, regardless of your age and experience, you may find that you don't need to be a mentor during this time in your life, you may need to be a mentee and have someone provide you with good advice and a clearer direction. This is something that you need to consider seriously.

Working with a mentee can fundamentally change your life. When you step into the role of a mentor, you start to consider your personal decisions, and you want the mentee to make the best decisions and become better than you. You will start to manage the relationship off of experience, rather than happenstance. Your mentee will encounter different challenges, many of which you will have experienced and can provide them with guidance and understanding on how to navigate certain situations. There will be circumstances or situations where you have no idea how to handle, either because you never experienced it or never thought that a person this age would want to consider or have to deal with. This part can get tricky because no one wants to steer someone in the wrong direction or react as if it's impossible to even want to consider "something" so unlikely. Remember, everyone has a story and a background that may be similar or different, never judge your mentee's story or activity, and always pivot back to "placing your feet in their shoes." Times like these are likely to occur when you don't have experience, and your response comes not from experience or observation, maybe from asking other mentors or reading articles that pertain to this situation. My goal is not to share with you all the easy parts of being a mentor, but the uncomfortable as well. Seriously consider this mentoring opportunity, but first look in the mirror and ask yourself, **AM I READY?**

There are multiple paths to becoming a mentor. The method that is highlighted or highly preferred for safety reasons and effective matchmaking purposes are through organizations that focus on mentorship. I will provide you with some helpful insights on the way in which large organizations that are dedicated to mentoring typically manage their mentoring processes. There are guidelines to follow when becoming a mentor through an organization such as: Big Brother, Big Sister, YWCA, Boys & Girls Club of America, Mentor, Imentor, My Brother's Keeper, Young Men's Initiative, and lots more. Some steps may differ per organization, but here is a general guide on how to become a committed mentor through proper protocol.

1. Seek mentoring opportunities through the following avenues:

a) Schools (colleges and universities) - Peer mentoring is established.

b) Nonprofit mentoring organizations within your community (i.e. *A Legacy Left Behind, Inc.*)

c) Community Centers Mentoring After School Programs.

d) Churches/Religious Organizations.

This process is self-volunteer, once you decide that the commitment is for you, then seek out organizations and start the process. The hardest part is you agreeing with yourself that you are ready for this responsibility. Once this is established, list out all the community organizations in your area. Finding an organization near your place of residence will help sustain commitment in attending weekend sessions and activity, rather than finding organizations that are far from you.

2. **Express an Interest**. Attend an orientation or call to speak to a representative for more information about the mentoring program. Request information on the requirements of the commitment process. Commitment is a big deal when applying to sign up with an organization, or should I say period. Many organizations vary on the commitment part, so asking this question first can determine if that organization is the best fit for you. Some mentoring organizations will tell you that you have to be committed to the mentee for at least 2 years and/or be committed to the program, which entitles no moving out of state. If you are in transition to starting school or a new career which means, leaving the state, then I would advise you to mentor somewhere in the state you will be living. Other organizations will pair you with virtual mentees, which allows you to be a mentor through virtual access. This service is not always favored, but it well exists. The goal of mentoring organizations as it pertains to commitment is that all encourage and strive for long-lasting relationships.

3. *The Application Process. The application process is mandatory for youth mentoring organizations (not so much

for job mentoring or informal mentoring). However, it is a process that requires basic information about yourself and your hobbies. This application is considered, "The Match-Maker" guide. Decisions are made based on your education, occupation, hobbies, location, gender, activities, etc., and mentor organizations work to find commonalities between you and a possible mentee. As you fill out an application, a parent of the mentee that they are signing up for this program is to fill out the application too. The best part of the application is that based on your interest age group level, you get to choose what age group works for you. Through the self-evaluation process, knowing your preferred age group that you can understand, commit to, and feel like you can give and relate more to is your choice. Working with organizations (i.e. nonprofits), this application also provides "what would you do" scenarios to help you get familiar with the process. The scenarios are important based on your responses because it shows your experience, your thought process, and your determination to guide the mentee to the right path. The application (due to the high volume of mentors needed and verifying of background checks) can take up to an average of 2-8 weeks before you are notified. For example, Imentor, an organization that focuses on building mentoring relationships that help low-income students graduate high school and succeed in college, has a 4-6 week application process that includes a mandatory 2- hour training. The trainings are designed to help the mentor understand what is appropriate and what is not appropriate in the mentoring experience. After the training, prospective mentors go through a screening process that includes a background check, fingerprinting, a phone interview, and an interview with a reference.[9] Mentor training is another way programs ensure safety, commitment, and that their volunteers will be fully evaluated and prepared for their role with a mentee. According to YWCA EmpowerGirlz Mentoring and Leadership Program, serves girls between the ages of 7 – 17; their application process can take up to 3-4 weeks. The outline that is used to determine if you are a qualified mentor is through their checklist:

Application Received	Mentor Contract	Mentor Matching Questionnaire	Health Clearance	HIPAA	Photo Release	Optional Form	Entered in Database	Interview Complete	Background Check Completed	Attended Orientation

Going through an organization is very necessary when it comes to pairing strangers together and building lasting relationships. Many ways that organizations address the diverse and complex needs of youth and informing mentors is received through specific training with clear expectations. For example, training mentors with a focus on cultural sensitivity and the negative impacts of ending mentoring relationships early may be necessary to help mentors working with immigrant youth and youth dealing with incarcerated parents. Immigrant youth are often working to adjust to a new culture and enduring misunderstandings related to their culture, Mentors of children with incarcerated parents may need training focused on how to deal with their mentees' feelings of embarrassment around their parent's incarceration and other challenges they may be facing. This was my experience after joining the organization: Imentor, a mentoring organization that builds mentoring relationships that empower first-generation students from low-income communities and pairs them with college-careered mentors. Imentor was the initial stage for me to pursue mentorship while in college. Giving back and inspiring someone else to make better decisions than I did was extremely rewarding. However, I was not ready for that responsibility. I was paired with a 9th-grade student whom I would meet with once a week at her school. Imentor and the school made an arrangement where one class period a week was set aside for mentor-mentee building time. This was mandated, because if the mentor did not come, then you had one mentee left alone while every other student was paired with their mentor, unless the notice of absence was submitted in advance. The initiation was tough because she felt as if I was not the right person for her. This was that culture shift, I was twenty years old at the time, and she didn't feel like I had much to offer her. There were commonalities, such as she attended a STEM high school and I had recently earned my Bachelor of Science degree in mathematics. However, what she wanted was a connection that I did not know how to provide at the initiation phase. After several trainings with the program and meetings with my mentee, we engaged in a closer relationship. We had more to communicate about, but I was not as open to her as she was with me. I was allowing her to share her life with me, which made me a good listener, but I did not share much of my personal life with her, which made her feel like I was not transparent. This was when I learned that mentoring is a two-way street. As a mentor, your mentee wants to know that as he/she pours out to you, you will pour out in return. This mentor-mentee relationship did not last long, my mentee ended up leaving the program, and I lost the desire to be partnered with a new mentee right away. I made efforts to reach out to her outside of the program, but her number changed and we lost touch. I realized that I did not establish a relationship with her parents, whom she did not often mention during our meetings. As I found out later that her parents were incarcerated and she was living with her grandparents.

4. **Acceptance.** Once your application has been approved, you are permitted to have an assigned mentee. This acceptance shows that you best fit a mentee in that program that asked for certain characteristics and you match that profile. This is a stage that shows that not only do you feel that you are capable of being a mentor, but an organization feels the same way. Once you are accepted, a handbook or a manual mentor guide for that organization will be given to you. A pledge or promise will be shared, and you will be asked to repeat it and sign it.

5. **Match Maker.** Mentoring is about establishing mutually beneficial partnerships between individuals to achieve specific goals. Reason being, matching mentors and mentees successfully will be one of the most critical aspects of the mentoring experience because the biggest obstacle is the difficulty, and sometimes awkwardness, of making a match between mentor and mentee who have one thing in common or nothing at all. Most organizations match based on the

mentee's needs and wants. If a professional mentee's application states that he/she wants a mentor who works in sports, then the decision committee will pull all applicants that reference having sports hobbies and careers in the sports industry.

Considerations for Matching for Organizations

- Comprehensive assessments of families, mentees and mentors, parent/guardian approval.
- Common interests (i.e., vocational, educational, and recreational).
- Goals for the mentee: educational enrichment, self-esteem enhancement, cultural enrichment, family and peer relationship improvement.
- Childhood upbringing, culture, and religion.
- Life experiences: absence of parent in household, growing up as the oldest child in a large family, death of a parent, raised by a grandparent.
- Expressed preferences: Race, gender, culture, sexual orientation, and age.

Questions and Scenarios

Scenario One- *Commitment*

You recently received your acceptance in joining a mentoring organization to become a more engaged citizen, and the organization says the commitment is one year to a high school student without moving to another state. Another requirement is that you must commit to two Saturdays in a month to meet your mentee at the programs office for five hours and commit to spending time and bonding outside of the space. With your new mentee, you will engage with their studies, expose them to new things, and share your successes with them.

Would you agree with this commitment? Why?

_____

_____

_____

_____

_____

_____

Scenario Two- *Match Making*

The matching process is complete, and you and your mentee hit it off right away. You were excited about your match until a few weeks ago when your mentee started calling you a few times a day during work hours and now the different times at night when you're home. You were excited that he/she likes you so much, but are unsure if the amount of time you are spending on the phone is appropriate and you don't want to hurt his/her feelings.

What should you do?

_____

_____

_____

_____

_____

Scenario Three- *Role Model*

You are out at a local club with some friends having a great time. You have been really stressed lately, working really hard to meet all of your obligations and you need to blow off some steam. You look over and see your mentee who is under age, but happens to have been admitted into this club. You realize that you're supposed to serve as a role model for him/her, but you're pretty drunk. Also, they are under age and should not be there. You have already begun to establish a trusting relationship with them as well as their parents.

How do you handle the situation? What do you say to him/her and when do you say it; the next day?

_____

_____

_____

_____

_____

What type of person do you ideally want to mentor Do you want someone with the same hobbies or the same career path interest?

_____

_____

_____

_____

_____

Are you ready to become a mentor?

_____

_____

_____

_____

_____

I would love to read your responses! Feel free to submit your answers to _felicia.onestepcloser@gmail.com_ so that I can give you a shout out.

CHAPTER 2: THE BUILD

When developing a mentoring partnership, make sure you have clear boundaries of what you can and cannot do for the mentee. A boundary can be thought of as a protective barrier that limits dos and don'ts in a partnership. For boundaries to be effective, they need to be applied on a consistent and ongoing basis. For example, when I am around my mentees, they know that I do not tolerate music with curse words, so if I am driving and they would like to control the radio station or listen to their music, it has to be the clean version. This was a boundary that I put in place during the initiation of our building stage. Another example is when my mentor told me not to cancel our outings the day of because she would have to travel a good distance to spend time with me and it would be an inconvenience if I cancelled within a short notice of time. This was a guideline that my mentor created to identify reasonable ways for me to behave toward her time and commitment without seeing her respond or react once that boundary was crossed.

The Build phase refers to identified strategies that both the mentor and the mentee set for building and sustaining a successful mentoring relationship. During The

THE BUILD

Build, each party states his/her likes, dislikes, "dos" and "don'ts." It is important for the mentor to set the tone at this stage. Creating a relationship of trust, clearly defining roles and responsibilities (boundaries), establishing short and long-term goals, interpersonal communication skills, exhibiting passion and openness, maintaining confidentiality, adaptability, availability, and collaboratively solving problems are critical components in the building process when strategizing on how to build an effective foundation. When building a house that you want to last, you don't rush through the beginning stages, which is the most impactful stage, you take your time and lay every piece in its proper position. Rushing through the building stage in the mentor-mentee relationship will become a weak foundation and would not last long. Follow these components and foundational structure for building a lasting relationship with your mentee.

Establishing Trust

Trust is established when a mentor gives off themselves more than the mentee can expect. For example, sharing life experiences and showing that failures happen to the best of them. The day trust was established with one of my mentees that was struggling in school, was when I shared

48

a failing grade that I received while I was in school on the same subject. This allowed my mentee to see that I am not perfect, that I am transparent and candid and that life is not over. Trust does not have to be kindled by a test of keeping secrets, it can be anything simple. Trust is considered a characteristic trait that represents one aspect of a person's behavior and attitude that makes up a person's personality.

Some mentees may be nervous about working with a mentor, so to put them at ease, you must create a trusting relationship by empathizing with their challenges, sharing knowledge without being patronizing, and remaining nonjudgmental. Just like Planet Fitness, the national fitness center, they believe in "No Judgment Zone," where people come and workout freely. This has proven lasting memberships and consistency, which is what we want from our relationships when building trust.

The following list provides some ideas for how the mentor can build trust with the mentee:

- Acknowledge your mentee's strengths and accomplishments from the outset of the mentoring process.
- Encourage questions of any type, and tell the mentee that there is no such thing as a bad question.

- Remember your mentee's big moments; such as birthdays, prom, games, performances, and more.
- Ask for and be open to receiving feedback from mentees when given; apply constructive feedback to improve mentoring skills.

Roles and Responsibilities

Roles in a mentor-mentee relationship are well defined throughout this book and should be clearly modeled within your mentoring relationship. As a mentor you are the leader, you are the convener and motivator. You have a concrete goal within your role, and that is to share knowledge, empower them, and see them through their transitional period whether that is junior high school to high school or high school to college. You are their path to success, not to say that they don't have internal role models in their families, but you are there for that purpose. Responsibility is a word that can be a misconception because as a mentor, why are you responsible for someone else's child? I know, think of it as a positive, you are reliable for helping that mentee get into college, you are one of the people that helped that mentee achieve his goals. It allows you to reap the credits and results. You did not give up on the mentee, so therefore they can acknowledge you in their achievements. It then becomes a win-win.

Short and Long-term Goals

This becomes a conversation starter; it can be your initial conversation or second conversation. This is where you can see what the mentee thinks and their outlook for the relationship, do they feel it's worth it? Do they know what to expect? Sharing five short and long-term goals with one another can assist with meeting the mentee's expectation. Goals overall is important, so getting your mentee in the habit, if they are not already, of writing out quarterly or annual goals for school, career, or personal development is excellent. There is a slight difference between the two; a short term goal is something that you want to accomplish in the next day or year term. A long term goal is the opposite; it can take over a year, a target area that is projected to require significantly more time for completion. When constructing your goals, make sure you utilize the effective acronym SMART, specific, measurable, attainable, realistic, and time-bound. SMART goal-setting brings structure and accountability into your goals and objectives.

Interpersonal Communication

Interpersonal communication is a verbal and nonverbal sharing of information between two or more persons. Mentees learn best from mentors who are sincere in their approach. First impressions are everything, based on your body language, mentees can sense if you are dedicated versus here to say you gave back to your community. Remember, people often remember more about *how* a subject is communicated than the speaker's knowledge of the subject. How are you communicating your mentor role?

There are two types of communication: verbal and nonverbal. Verbal communication is the communication that occurs through spoken words, such as hello, or I am happy to be here today. Nonverbal communication is when communication occurs through unspoken mediums, such as gestures, posture, facial expressions, silence, and eye contact. It's not just that you said, "I am happy to be here today," but did your body language express that same feeling? It is important for mentors to remember that they are communicating to mentees when they are speaking *and* when they are not speaking. In fact, up to 93% of human communication is nonverbal.[10] This includes body language, which tells those with whom we are communicating a great deal about what we are thinking and feeling.

---

[10] Mehrabian, Albert. Nonverbal communication. Chicago: Aldine-Atherton, Chicago; 1972.

Examples of positive or open body language include:

- Eye contact (depending on the culture)
- Open or relaxed posture
- Nodding or other affirmation
- Pleasant facial expressions
- Standing positions (i.e. folding of the arms can signal; not interested in communication)

It is important for you to identify the nonverbal cues that your mentee gives so that you can better understand how to approach him/her, particularly if he/she does not feel like speaking on a certain situation. Everyone has a bad day, even mentors, so make sure that communication is shared. Be honest and open with your mentee when you don't feel like meeting or you have to cancel a date because you don't feel like connecting. Don't connect and give off a bad vibe. Mentees are depending on you. Some of them may need to be removed from a negative environment for a few hours, thus their time with you is important and impactful. Others are simply depending on a continual development of the mentor-mentee relationship. Sometimes you are considered their one-way ticket to success.

I remember committing to a date with my mentee early one morning and as my day began—which included going to work, and dealing with bosses and relationships, I just wanted to go home and shut down. I did not want to deny our visit because I knew the type of environment she was heading to, so I decided to hang out anyway, but I was not fully attentive and she noticed. She was visibly upset because she thought that she did something wrong, or that I simply was not interested in being with her. I never communicated my issues with her, but she perceived these things based on my body language and gestures. Make sure that communication is something that you manage, this is a part of the building phase. Once the communication is good, then the passion for the relationship begins to unfold.

Passion

Mentees are aware and will notice if you are just spending time to prove to your organization that you're giving back to your community. They can tell if you're just trying to boost your resume. Make sure you authentically demonstrate that you're passionate about helping and being in your mentee's life. Remember, it shows through your tone and body expressions whether you're passionate or just going through the motions. Passion can be noticed through your actions. Are you staying committed to your scheduled outings? Do you make yourself available or is your schedule too busy to fit in time with the mentee? Do you spend time with and try to get to know your mentee's family members? People don't care how much you know until they know how much you care. This too goes with mentees. Show them that you care through your actions and you will reap the reward of your efforts.

Openness

Maintaining transparency is huge. You don't want your mentee feeling like you're a lawyer or social worker and you're just taking notes while they pour their feelings and most intimate stories on you. You have to share information about you as well. And be open to discussing topics with your mentee. I remember when both of my mentees shared very personal information with me and I couldn't understand how they could have gone through such trying experiences at such a young age, but I then had to remember my situation and how I was brought up. I shared my story with them, and they gravitated to me more because, one I was open, and two they knew I could relate. Being relatable and open when appropriate practically helps the building process with your mentee. Remember, this mentor–mentee relationship is a two-way street. In order to build effectively and grow the relationship, there is something that you will have to give as well.

Confidentiality

What is considered confidential can be tricky when building a relationship with your mentee. The goal is that you want your mentee to be able to confide in you, but you do not want to take the place of the mentee's internal guardian. Confidentiality refers to the mentor's duty to maintain trust and to respect the privacy of the mentee. If your mentee gave you a choice as to whether they can tell their secrets to their friends or you, which would you chose? Without appropriate confidentiality, mentors will find that it is very difficult, if not impossible, to establish trust and build rapport with their mentees. Note that at the beginning of the mentoring relationship, it is very important for the mentor to explain to the mentee any circumstances in which confidentiality may be broken. Such circumstances include when a mentee's life is in danger, or if the mentee is engaging in illegal activity. If this is the case, try to get as much information from your mentee to avoid them from moving forward, keep them close and always report it back to their parents so that they can handle the situation.

To maintain confidentiality with their mentees, mentors need to be sensitive to when and where conversations should be held and never leave information sitting with providing feedback to your mentee. Some mentees may feel ashamed if they are corrected in front of their siblings or peers, so make efforts to offer feedback in a private setting whenever possible. Additionally, the mentor should refrain from sharing details of mentor-mentee conversations with the mentee's superiors until a more appropriate time. Confidentiality is of particular importance when the mentor-mentee pairing does not match traditional cultural hierarchies. For example, ensuring confidentiality is especially critical when the mentor and mentee are not of the same gender, the mentor is younger than the mentee, the mentor is of a different career aspiration, the mentor is from a different ethnic group, the mentor has a different sexual orientation than the mentee, or the mentor does not have the same religious views as the mentee. In these situations, mentoring can still be a positive learning experience for both parties. Establishing a relationship in which confidentiality is a top priority can help alleviate any tensions associated with such differences between the mentor and mentee such as the ones above. Mentors should not promise the mentee that all confidential information will be kept amongst the relationship. This is a trap and a breaking of the building process when a mentor commits to this.

Adaptability

"Speak truth into younger men and women. Be willing to share opportunities. Don't cling to your own knowledge, skill set or ambition. Don't fear the word mentor. Share what you do, what you know, and who you follow," stated advice from Sheryl Sandberg, Chief Operating Officer of Facebook and the New York Times Bestselling author of *Lean In*. Mentors must adapt to the notion that they have been called to support and to mentor those that are coming up behind them. Adaptability is the skill of responding to changing circumstances and coping with the transition effectively. Being adaptable requires you to fit into a new environment quickly and easily. Mentors must be an adaptable and a reliable source for their mentees. As a mentor, you have to become open-minded to doing, hearing, and observing different activities that your mentee may consider. If you and your mentee are the opposite genders, try putting yourself in his or her shoes. Try to understand what they might be experiencing.

For example, if you are a female mentoring a young male you have to understand the hormonal shifts of young males, such as acne, hair growth, deep voice tone, relationship views, and their many obsessions with things like clothing, sneakers, and electronics. You have to understand their penmanship and organizational skills. Acknowledge that there may be a difference in how you do things and offer suggestions. Never invoke that they need to fix something that is the norm for them because you don't want to come off as a dictator. Their knowledge is ever-evolving, but you can assist with improving and sharpening their skills by asking, understanding, and accepting where they are in the developmental process. Mentors paired with mentees of different socioeconomic status require a certain level of understanding as well.

It is impossible to mentor a person effectively without understanding the person's needs. Not all mentees will require the same style of mentoring. Some mentees will need more direction than others, and other mentees may not need direction as much as they would need assistance building up confidence to follow a path they have already decided on. The mentor-mentee relationship is a bridge builder that comes in handy when trying to establish a connection between two different generations and backgrounds. In the poem called Bridge Builders by Will Allen Dromgoole, there was a man that decided to build a bridge after surviving a deep wave when sailing. Many bystanders that saw that he wanted to go back into that deep sea and build a bridge "to span the tide" said that he was "wasting his strength building here" since that day was breaking into evening and the tide was becoming deeper. He was determined to build this bridge no matter what because "there followed after me today a youth whose feet must pass this way. This stream that has been naught to me, he too, must cross... I am building this bridge for him!" This is what the mentor-mentee relationship is about, building a better path to make it a little easier for your mentee to cross.

Availability

To build a quality mentor-mentee relationship, the two must agree on a schedule that they both can commit to in order to maintain balance. Mentors are especially looked upon to establish ground rules as far as their availability. Since many mentors are older, they are the ones with a set schedule, so committing to established time is a process that the mentor should initiate and manage. Many organizations do not place a time limit or a commitment schedule on mentors as to when they should be available, but make sure you commit to seeing or speaking to your mentee several times a month. In many formalized mentoring partnerships, your availability carries significant weight when an organization is considering choosing you to become a mentor. Most mentoring organizations will consider a potential mentor with the most availability rather than someone who has only a few spaces open on their weekly schedule. Flexibility as a mentor is also an important asset and can help build the relationship faster. Availability does not just satisfy actual time, but giving of advice. As a mentor, you may not have experienced a smooth building process like the one given, you may have shared most of your stories, and your mentee may not have opened up to you right away, but I am telling you the time will come. When the time does come, that is when you must be available to listen and offer advice or just a hug.

Problem Solving

It takes a Now Generation mentor to get to the Now Generation mentee (youth). In this new era, youth are dealing with more than an ordinary mentor can handle, let alone a teacher or a single parent. We all have to work together to build the mentee to be the next generation leader. NOW stands for New Obstacles to Worry, this generation of mentees are dealing with different stumbling blocks that as a mentor we would not even think. This generation is going through depression, peer pressure, abuse, lack of support at home, bullying, drugs and alcohol, dating, sexual orientation acceptance, and lack of education. How can we reach these mentees who are going through multiple stumbling blocks at the same time? The answer is we have to empower them, by not focusing on their wrongs, but solving problems through determination, commitment, honesty, and love. As a mentor, our role is not to lecture them on their wrongs or hold them accountable for their actions, but to help them to see that "you" as a mentor was no different from them. Showing them that nothing new is happening NOW that did not take place before. Every youth (mentee) feels as if they are the only ones dealing with these stumbling blocks and no one can understand their hurt and distress. As a mentor, this is your chance to be REAL to them and become vulnerable, share your story, share your struggle, and show them you love them. Love is the greatest commandment and the strongest medicine, it heals and restores relationships. We are not in our mentee's life to command, discourage, judge, criticize, interrogate, and discount their decisions, we are not their parents or the sole authority figure in their life, we are problem solvers, we want to build a trusting relationship so that the mentee can tell us all the things that we need to know before they confide in their friend's advice. Our job here is to show support, console, and sympathize, convincing our mentee that the problems that they are encountering are not as bad, and we are here to help them look at the bright side of things. For example, if your mentee is sad because they were just dumped by their significant other, instead of telling them to "get over it, you're still young and you have time to focus on the opposite sex or same sex," show vulnerability by saying you were dumped multiple times at the same age and explain the steps you took to overcome the breakup. Share funny stories of how you stayed up all night and cried or the time you prank-called your "ex" to see if they would answer. These stories will help with relief and build a stronger mentor-mentee relationship bond. You can share funny math jokes, such as, "Dear Algebra, stop asking us to find your X, she's not coming back" to lighten up the mood because everyone wants to hear about math.

CHAPTER 3: CONFRONT PRO-SEQUENCES

Pro-sequence is a strategic new term used to gather information from a youth or individual to avoid wall-building. Instead of approaching a mentee with a consequence (wrong choices or decisions made) that a parent told you something that they would like for you to confront your mentee (their child) on, you will approach them with a positive first. "Pro" is the prefix meaning positive, when an individual hears the word consequence, it's a derogatory word, it speaks to negative, trouble, and they immediately build a wall. "Con" is the prefix which means negative, in order to gather information from your mentee, you have to come to them from a positive approach. A sequence is the order of steps, many teenagers have a mindset of trying things on their own, and we've all done it. The pro-sequence strategy is taking the order of steps that the mentee did that caused them to get in trouble or not in compliance with their parent's rules; you will approach the steps from a positive view and offer their opinions on how they could turn their sequence around. Mark Evans, DM (Deal Maker) owns and operates a massive real estate empire, bestselling author, blogger, and believer in mentorship. He wrote on his blog about the comparison of mentorship and investing, "Being a mentor is like making an investment: you need to consider the positives, negatives, and risks." There will ultimately be challenges that confront the mentor/mentee relationship. The mentor may not be available to attend their mentee performances, games, or big events. There will be times when the mentee is not performing at his/her best, and the parents are having difficulty getting through to them, and then you step in and rather than things getting better, they get worse. This is where many mentors throw in the towel and give up.

I was in this boat before, where I could not understand the shift that occurred with my mentee. I had been building a relationship with her since she was 11 years old. In her transition to adolescence, she began "smelling" herself like most teenagers do, and all of a sudden she didn't see the need for having a mentor. Smelling oneself is when someone feels they do not have to follow order and that friends and independence matter most. What do you do? Well as a mentor, you stay and work through the transition that your mentee is experiencing. Then you praise them for their boldness to want to be independent, then you listen.

There comes a time when you have to praise a person instead of reprimanding them. As a professional tutor, I've noticed that a child will break down or close themselves off when their parent is yelling at them and disciplining them for their lack of improvement or misbehavior in school. I've experimented with this myself. More importantly, research demonstrates that when a child is being praised or given more attention for the good that they do rather than the bad, that's when improvements occur. Mentoring through consequences are the same thing, instead of focusing on the bad that they are doing, strategize a better approach by concentrating on the Pro-sequence. When a mentee is disrespecting their parents' authority or failing in school, or whatever the situation is, as a mentor, your role is to guide and advise the mentee through communication and transparency. So instead of telling them about the consequences (wrongs) and what they should have done differently, share what they did right in the situation, praise them that you noticed that they did not argue back to their authority figure this time. Share how they raised their homework grade from last semester to current, they may still have failed the course, but praise their effort for approaching it differently.

When communicating, make sure to share with your mentee what they did right in a particular situation and get feedback from the mentee on why they thought their behavior was favorable. Be transparent and authentic when discussing these issues. Share some stories of your past and how you made mistakes, but how things could've been different if you had a mentor to guide you. *Con* is a connotation to be negative, and *Pro* is denoted as a positive reference, reinforce this knowledge on your mentee. People or should I say humans regurgitate toward positive and like the subject physics, when a positive is placed with a negative it magnetically pulls toward the positive and attracts. Even if your mentee may appear to be going down the wrong road, remind them about their wins and positive attributes—offer praises, and initially the positives will outweigh the negatives. Like the saying, if you let a dog roam, it will find its way home." Similarly, in biblical scriptures, both the prodigal son and the lost sheep went astray for a period, but eventually returned home to open arms. Provide that same safe and caring space for your mentee, and they will eventually come to their senses.

This pro-sequence strategy can work in all categories because remember, we are dealing with the Now Generation and they have a lot of weight that they are carrying on their shoulders. A part of the mentor-mentee relationship is to break down the walls that they may have rising.

The Attachment- Show yourself approved

"Success begets success." - Unknown

Future generations are counting on your help, and as mentioned earlier, every successful person has a mentor. Once you build a relationship and the mentee can depend on you with personal information, then the trust has been captured. This is when the attachment happens. On average, it takes about 10 – 24 months for a true mentor-mentee relationship to establish an attachment phase. As a mentor, you need to be mindful of this, as you don't want to start something then end it in the early stages of growth. Mentees do become attached to the idea that someone other than their family member supports them and believes in their success. This is a vital component along with the building phase because the purpose of a mentor-mentee relationship is to attach and establish a long-lasting relationship. As a mentor, your goal is not to take the place of a parent, best friend or a sibling, but establish a close relationship to get to know the mentee personally and professionally.

There is no limit to the amount of information that should be disclosed or withheld, but always open up as best as you can. Moreover, the experience of trusting and having a close relationship with your mentee may lead the mentee to develop positive expectations about interpersonal relationships with others, which in turn can promote positive relationships. This leads to the mentee finding their life's purpose and down a path to the road of success.

Establishing a trusting mentoring relationship helps to promote career success. Mentors can impart specific knowledge and expertise which contributes to a mentee's learning and skill development. Mentors can also facilitate professional networking by introducing mentees to influential individuals within academic, community, and organizational contexts. These important career (professional) channels can in turn lead to career success and competitive advantage among their peers and counterparts. Whether it's in receiving a job experience at an early age, enhancing their resume skills through outstanding performance, receiving college scholarships without research and/or receiving more mentors; thus all involves around adding to a mentee's development.

My mentees and I formed a strong attachment that not only includes working to improve their personal and professional skills, but they have also helped to develop me professionally as well. When I launched my business, one of my mentees was able to market my business for me, which helped to bring in additional clientele and he was able to use this skill on his resume as a result of his marketing experience. My other mentee helped with building my summer externship program by both coming up with the idea and building the platform. This skill allowed her to place on her resume as a task "assist in building new initiatives." The attachment phase is a win-win for both the mentee and the mentor. The more you build, share, confront pro-sequences, and communicate honestly, the better the results will show. Success begets success—not only will the mentee receive the benefits from the mentoring experience, but so will the mentor.

Another part of the attachment phase is *clinging*, when a mentor-mentee relationship becomes more like a personal relationship. This happens when the mentee starts to see the mentor as an older sibling or parental figure and the mentor begins to view the mentee as a daughter or younger sibling. The major cause of this is when there is a lack of personal relationships in the lives of either the mentor or mentee. For instance, the bond that my mentor (Ms. Lucretia Glover) and I established shifted from academic mentoring to workplace mentoring, then to a personal mother-daughter type of relationship. This manifested due to my lack of stable parenting and support, not only as a young child but as an adult. In the case of my mentor, not having children of her own at that time created a bond that grew beyond any level we both could have imagined. Don't be alarmed if your mentoring relationship starts to grow into a personal attachment; it just means you have connected with your mentee in a way that no one has ever connected with them before. Embrace it as them filling a void that is valuable to your personal life for this particular moment in time. This can also be managed and monitored by setting boundaries and not allowing this phase to get this far. Another point to consider when a mentor is becoming overly attached to the mentee and family, it is especially difficult for a young person to move on. As a mentor, ask yourself whether you are willing to take on the emotional challenge of getting involved with a child and then, when it is time, letting go. Whether the letting go is temporary (they are away in school, or studying abroad or military) to permanent, they just decided to move on and grow.

CHAPTER 4: PARENT - MENTOR RELATIONSHIP

If anyone wants to be a mentor to an adolescent, the priority is to solicit the permission of their parent(s) or guardian. The friendship that is developed between a mentor and mentee is a special relationship just for them, but parents have an important role in helping that relationship to be successful. As mentioned earlier, mentoring offers a number of benefits. One of these benefits is an improved relationship between the mentee and his/her parents.[11]

The involvement of parents is essential, however in this day and age, parents are extremely busy, working or catering to multiple children. As a result, many parents miss out on mentoring opportunities because they simply lack the information, the whereabouts, and the understanding of the role. Mentoring opportunities usually are presented to parents when they are surrounded by other parents whose children are benefiting from mentoring or by way of schools that provide a

---

[11] Authors: Patti MacRae & Michael Garringer 2006 Adapted by: Rebekah Holbrook, Virginia Mentoring Partnership 2012: http://www.vamentoring.org/images/uploads/wysiwyg/VMP_Parent_Guide_to_Mentoring_P rograms.pdf

list of youth resources. Many working parents would find value in allowing their youth to be mentored by someone who is closer in age to their child, and with whom the child can better relate to. However, the reality is that some parents may feel threatened by another adult in their child's life. This is quite understandable; there are a lot of crazy and complicated things that are happening in this world, let alone their environment. So, if a parent is hesitant, or there are points of contention with parents as many of them are unaware of the benefits of having a mentor in their child's life can bring, make sure you're understanding and offer to answer all questions and concerns immediately. One of the duties of a parent is to protect their child from any hurt, harm or danger, and not just to hand over their child to any stranger.

Parents need to understand and be comfortable with the role of a mentor. Mentors are not meant to replace the parent, and it must be made clear that they are there to be a guide and a friend rather than to take on a parental or authoritative role. Parents do need to be mindful, especially when a mentor-mentee relationship has stored up trust, the mentee will confide in the mentor before they confide in the parent. On topics such as bullying and being uncomfortable, school-related work or behaviors, a performance that the mentee may be nervous about, and a specific relationship or sexual encounters, are all issues that an adolescent may face, but may not immediately choose to share with a parent. Once the parent agrees to allow a mentoring relationship, there is a balancing act that must occur between the mentor and parent. As a parent, it is important that you communicate with your child's mentor about certain conversations that may take place and how you would like them to respond. It is important for mentors to occasionally reiterate to the parent the purpose of their role as a mentor in the life of their mentee (youth).

How to Find a Mentor

Parents are encouraged to pursue a mentor for their child through their own networks. Many community leaders are open and willing to have the privilege of becoming your child's mentor. All it takes is a simple ask whether it's through a networking event such as a conference, or through a personal text message showing/expressing interest. However, simply because you've expressed an interest does not mean that you shouldn't arrange a formal meeting and introduction identifying specific rules (boundaries) and desires for this new relationship with your child. Also, include a specific timeframe for the length of the mentorship. Many may ask if the child (mentee) has a say in this matching process. As an expert, I would say yes; every child should be able to approve and provide their input when identifying a match or mentor. Whether it's asking questions like, "What should I as your mentee expect to get out of this relationship that my parent(s) are not able to provide?" With this particular question and others, it can allow the mentor to prove their passion and long-term objectives with your child.

Parents should also remember that when looking at community leaders and prospects to engage, they may have limited time to commit due to other obligations, or they may already have mentees that they are working with. What I am proposing is to also consider a rejection due to these constraints.

Another alternative, just in case you don't have positive leaders in your community or gatherings that you feel would be a great fit for your child, as stated in the beginning, search for mentoring organizations. The first place to start is from your child's school, ask for a list of youth centers and organizations. With this resource, you will be able to begin a safer search because all of the organizations listed would have been vetted by the Department of Education and other government agencies that perform and audit background checks when working with youth under 24 years old.

What the Mentor is not

Remember that the mentor's role is to be there for your child, not for you personally or other children in your family unless specified and agreed upon. The mentor cannot become the parent's spy or take on the role of friend or counselor to the parent. Just as the youth and mentor need to develop trust, the mentor and parent also must have a trusting relationship. [12] The trusting relationship could insist on being honest and speaking honestly to one another, especially when it concerns the mentee.

Also, try not to recruit your child's mentor to your neighbor's kids or close family members. This can cause a conflict of interest or an interruption to the building phase with the mentor and mentee; one may feel left out or ignored. Try to avoid asking the mentor to take other siblings along on outings or to become a personal babysitter. I know this part is hard because once a relationship is establish, comfortability kicks in and no parent wants one child to receive all of the excitement and the other child(ren) are not. You may encourage the mentor to include the entire family, including you the parent when arranging mentor-mentee day. You may

---

[12] Mentored youth show improved relationships with parents. Posted on March 23, 2012 by Lisa Bottomley, Michigan State University Extension-
http://msue.anr.msu.edu/news/strengthening_youth_parent_relationships_through_mentoring

also recommend that the mentor provides a list of activities or bonding suggestions that you as the parent may use with your child(ren). Encourage your child to thank his/her mentor and show appreciation for the time they spend together. If your child is being "grounded," inform the mentor and see if you can arrange a meeting for the mentor to speak to the mentee. Assist with the building process and encourage your child to open up during this process.

Communication with the Mentor

Keep in mind some simple things such as letting the mentor know when you have a change of address, phone number, or other contact information, or if there is a significant change in your lives that may affect the relationship—such as moving away from the area or a loss in the family. Remember, this is a two-way relationship, if the mentor feels like the relationship is being abandoned, the mentor will disconnect. Another communication piece, if there is a special performance or graduation ceremony for the mentee and there are limited amounts of tickets, please inform the mentee that their mentor may not be able to attend. Missing this piece of information can cause distrust because what you probably don't know, is the mentee probably informed the mentor about this special event and invited them in advance. The mentor quickly responds with "I will defiantly be there," the mentee confirms with "you promise," and the mentor repeats with assurance, "yes." Meanwhile, the parent informs the mentor that there are not enough tickets or does not report the full information such as address, time, date, and attire. Overall, the mentee feels abandoned or hurt and begins to build a wall over the fact that the mentor did not keep their word. Please communicate with your child.

Be Open and Transparent

As a parent, you always have the right to withhold your child from specific activities that you do not want him participating in and can ask mentors not to express certain points of view to your child. Having this open dialogue can help build the mentor-parent relationship because it sets boundaries before occurrences happen. Disagreements hardly occur, but when you have a parent who fully doesn't agree or understand the benefit of their child having a mentor, sometimes discussions on values and interests may appear to be debated, which are common in any relationship. However, you should remember that two of the most valuable things a mentor provides are new experiences and different ideas.

Mentors broaden horizons by introducing their mentee to worlds that would not have been available otherwise. Remember, this is not to say that the parent is not capable of showing their child a different view of the world, but mentors can help with providing another lens.

Gift Giving and Monetary Transactions

As a rule, mentors are not encouraged to give gifts or spend money on activities. A mentor may purchase a small token gift to acknowledge a special occasion such as a birthday or achievement, but shopping, trips, and regular gifts of items or cash are not expectations. Parents should (if possible) provide funds for their child to expense during their outing with their mentor. Occasionally, mentors may treat their mentee to a lunch or soda, or pay for a special outing such as a trip to the movies or an art museum, but this is always at the discretion of the mentor, and should not be an expectation of the relationship, unless the mentor program policies say otherwise. Mentor programs typically encourage mentors to find low-cost or free activities to do with their mentees, such as hiking or cycling, going to a park, or visiting the public library. Of course, as a mentor, you want to go above and beyond for your mentee, especially if the resources for funding are low. However, the point about mentoring is the bonding piece and communication, not the amount of money that is spent. Parents, this part can become a lot easier if you can share with your child that mentors are not "pocket change" they are not here to give you the money that is in their pockets. Parents, we also do not encourage "IOUs" with the mentors, if the mentor is comfortable then proceed by your own discretion. As a mentor, we do not expect to be treated to dinner by the parent or to receive a holiday or birthday gift either, we don't expect it, but again by your own discretion based on the relationship, please proceed.

Know the Parental Role

Parent satisfaction with the quality of the mentoring relationship as well as their own relationship with the mentor has the potential to influence the relationship trajectory. Parent's roles vary as far as expectation, but here is a steady list of roles that parents take on when establishing and approving the mentor-mentee relationship.

> **Collaborators** are the types of parents who actively engages and coordinates with the mentor on scheduling, suggestion of activities, family surprises, and revealing their child's weaknesses.

➢ **Coaches** are certain types of parents who play the role of also mentoring the mentor. They have resources that are beneficial for the mentor to have. Sometimes mentors are college level and can use assistance in work-life balance, time management, and editing of term papers.

➢ **Mediators** are certain types of parents that step in when the mentoring relationship is struggling or need to be terminated, this particular parent sometimes intervenes in order to advocate for their child.

➢ **Liaisons** are certain types of parents that introduce the mentor benefits to other parents and schools. This parent introduces their child's mentors to people and organizations by praising the relationship between the mentor and mentee and highlighting the change that they see within their child from having a mentor, such as grades, communication, habits, and growth.

CHAPTER 5: MENTOR MODELS TESTIMONIALS

We can all agree that reading something is less effective than hearing testimonials from actual Mentor Models. Here we have actual mentors who share about the process and how it took place for them. Each mentor model experienced their mentorship relationship differently, which you will as well. No mentorship relationship will be the same, but here are unique stories about the building process and the effects that each encountered. Here are three mentor models from different backgrounds and schedules that made time and commitment to become a mentor and the benefits they received from becoming a mentor.

Felicia Fort

Professional Tutor, Professional Mentor, Accountant, Professor, Entrepreneur, and Speaker.

Through many mentoring experiences, I have embraced the saying, "If you examine any successful person they typically have one thing in common: they had a mentor." One of Maya Angelou's quotes that is dear to my heart and the reason why I continue to be a mentor and an advocate for mentorship is, "Success is liking yourself, liking what you do, and liking how you do it." Seeing my mentees and connecting with mentoring organizations regularly, and looking in the eyes of my mentees, I know that the mentorship experience is a successful and productive one—from growth to independence and development. Watching them graduate from high school and transition to college—it is a joy and an honor to be a part of the mentoring movement.

How does mentorship work, you may ask? Largely by building confidence – we share our past, and we place ourselves in the shoes of our mentees—knowing that outside of our relationship is a different world. Why do my mentees continue to call and confide in and boast about our relationship? Because trust was established by me proving "that I like what I do" and that I "CARE." I did not have a mentor until I entered college. I would have loved a mentor while still in junior high school because I was dealing with low self-esteem, not realizing the importance of education, but experiencing bullying, lack of attention at home, and not having a positive role model in my environment. Growing up in a household where I wasn't given the best advice on the high school application process, and understanding the difference between choosing a private, public, or boarding school that would best benefit my success- was difficult. My struggle while growing up was getting attention from my parents because they either had to work two jobs and had three other kids to pay attention to. The fact that this happened to me made me realize that other kids are experiencing "feeling left out" syndrome. I was eager to talk to anyone who paid me attention and who knew more about future resources than my family. I knew I needed someone, but whom?

Serving as a friend and role model to my mentees and other young girls has helped them to surmount overwhelming obstacles. The mentees that I work with are no different from any other youth or professional that may need a mentor. Age aside, there lies a commonality of wanting someone to "hear" them, lead them down the right path, and speak life into their situations. Most of the mentees I've worked with came from dysfunctional environments where all they see and hear is failure. While others come from great families, but still need someone to see them and see their normalcy. Many of my mentees see the struggle in their environments and home and have to be the optimistic one when everyone around them is a pessimist. I know that any mentorship experience and mentor program is very important for young minority girls and boys especially because it gives them a sense of acceptance, knowledge, and a dedicated mentor who's leading and encouraging them in the right path, while also having fun. Mentorship is a generational curse breaker. If many youths become active members in mentoring programs, I believe the high school dropout rate and teenage pregnancy rate will decrease, but we need mentors to step up, make time, and make the sacrifice to change a mentee's life. Mentoring programs and the mentorship experience provide valuable resources and knowledge that are not always available in underserved neighborhoods, such as programs on STEM education, teenage dating (healthy vs. unhealthy relationships), the high school search process, anti-bullying, financial success, scholarships, and anti-sex trafficking—just to name a few. All of these issues are prevalent in our local community, but opportunities are scarce when trying to gain insight.

I've been a mentor for the last 8 years, and the effect it has on me is indescribable, my mentees are now in college, and some are moving into the twelve grade, my longest mentees I had since they were 11 years old are now 18 years old. The beginning of this journey took time and patience, but most of all it took vulnerability from me to open up and to allow them to see that I am a real person and that I have flaws and failures as well. My building process took eleven months for each, and it took less time with their parents, which was an easy connection because they wanted a positive role model in their kids' lives. Overall, this mentorship experience showed me the true meaning of commitment. I would not change this for the world. Now I have six mentees that I am constantly checking on, and they are following up.

Sankaya Hall

Associate Director, Chapter Development at The National Society of Collegiate Scholars (NSCS).

Serving as a youth mentor provides me with the opportunity to change lives and transform the way youths think about life and their future. I find joy in helping my mentees not only stay in school, but also in building their confidence and instilling in them that they have what it takes to attend college as well. As someone who grew up in a poverty-stricken environment with very few positive influences, I love sharing my stories of adversity and how I overcame obstacles, along with new and diverse experiences of today. In return, it is a great feeling to see them embrace these new experiences. I also learn a lot from them— reminders to relax, be more appreciative and patient, in addition to new information they share with me. My experiences with them have truly enriched my life, and I feel blessed and thankful to have the opportunity to serve as a change agent in my own community. Now it was not like this at first, I did not want to feel like a babysitter and reliable for someone else's child, but when I had the opportunity to build with my mentee, it was more than what I expected. I was actually pouring into another human who took in everything that I shared and was thankful for the exposure when we went out and did different activities together. I also thought that it would affect or hinder my work-life balance due to my work schedule, I do not have a lot of *me* time or friend's time, but it actually helped me manage my time wisely and effectively. These youth just want another positive figure in their lives who listens and is real, being that I grew up in Detroit, I know all about "Realness" and listening.

Lucretia Glover

Mathematics educator and Doctoral student at Columbia University.

As an educator of over 13 years, I realize that educating students extends past the walls of a classroom. Although my interactions (i.e. good or bad) with students lends an ear to hearing the day to day issues that students face, as a reflective teacher, I am moved by my students' ability to adapt to situations—learning by doing and overcoming challenges.

Within the 13 years of teaching mathematics, my role as the teacher has sometimes crossed over to a co-parent, a mentor, and a counselor. Although I may not have been able to address all of my students' needs, my former students regularly inform me about how much my previous actions have helped to mold their lives. When asked to describe their teacher, they will more than likely say, "Oh, you don't want to play with Ms. Glover. You know she is not going to put up with foolishness." In being fair and honest, my students have made an accurate assessment of my personality. I am fair, I mean business, and I am all about not allowing students to make excuses about why they cannot achieve something.

Their follow-up comment would be something about me being the best teacher they know. Although I don't know if every student would agree with these comments, I feel confident in saying that I am always here for my students. I believe that I was put on earth to share my knowledge of math as well as life. Through my conversations with students, I hope that I will continue to be a part of their long journey. Whether it be the students I have mentored (i.e. Felicia, an undergraduate professor, educational nonprofit founder, and the author of this book; Patricia, a police officer; Timothy, a business leader and motivational speaker; or John, a current high school student destined for success) or the student I am soon to meet; I believe that my role as an educator is to truly be there for my students. In achieving this, I accept the challenge of walking alongside them on their journey to realizing their dreams. For that reason, the greatest gift that I have ever received is knowing that they have the ability to create change.

PART II:

THE MENTEE

ROLE

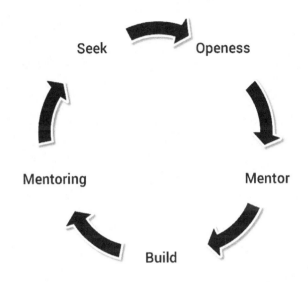

Seek

Openess

Mentoring

Mentor

Build

"Don't ask just anyone to be your mentor."

~Sheryl Sandberg

CHAPTER 6: WHAT IS A MENTEE

Webster's dictionary defines a *mentee* as a person who is advised, trained, or counseled by a mentor. Also known as a protégé, a french word meaning protected. Everyone is in need of a mentor, the question is: how can you become a mentee? A mentee is not classified as an underserved or underprivileged individual who is failing due to institutional injustice and school tracking systems or someone who doesn't have any good role models in their environment or family. A mentee is anyone who would like some guidance on a specific task or multiple tasks. CEO's of major corporations are often mentees or mentors.

For example, I knew I needed a mentor to help shape my professional development. I was a mathematics major in college and not sure of what career I wanted to pursue or how I needed to get there. I knew that I did not want to become a traditional classroom teacher, having to manage classrooms, students, and tests, but it was not clear to me what the options were. So I paired up with a mathematician at my college and started to communicate my desires and conundrums. I was completely transparent and open with my feelings. Then I started asking for advice and offering my assistance with anything she needed, and after about one month, I asked her to be my mentor. She was delighted, and she knew the commitment that she agreed to and she was ready to take on that commitment. Not only did she broaden my understanding of what I wanted to continue to achieve, but she helped me come to a conclusion of what I did not want to do. Where do we stand as mentees? In order to consider becoming a mentee, you have to ask yourself "Am I Ready?" The word mentee is gender-versal, it represents he or she.

David Nish the former CEO of Standard Life Insurance, an investment firm located in the United Kingdom and globally committed to helping individual's save on insurance, mentioned in a 2015 Harvard Business Review article that when he was promoted from CFO to CEO at Standard Life, he understood the scale of the challenge his company faced. The 185-year-old giant corporation had just embarked on a sweeping transformation from an insurer to a long-term savings and investment company. Nish also knew that as the person leading the change, he would be tested by decisions and management situations he hadn't encountered in the past. Nish decided to seek a mentor, someone who could show him the ropes of being a leader of a big corporation; he turned to adviser Niall FitzGerald, a former chairman of Unilever, another major corporation that deals with brands. The mentoring relationship they subsequently established was illustrative with those outside of their natural environments, but with similar goals such as educational, professional, and personal.

The Self-Evaluation Process

What do you want out of a mentoring relationship? A potential mentee should strongly consider what they are hoping to get out of this new relationship and share those hopes and expectations with their mentor. Before you get into these six models, it will be helpful to set the foundation by covering what's most important before committing to a mentoring relationship. What do they want out of it? What will they put into it? What are their fears? Mentees understand and realize that successful mentoring relationships do not necessarily happen automatically or overnight—rather that it's a process and the end result can lead to that of genuine engagement and sustained effort. Drawing upon my own experience and that of others, here are six models that every highly effective mentee should consider.

1) **It's all about the questions you ask.** Starting off this new relationship with another person can be someone surreal because in your mind you are not sure if they

are doing this for community service, a leadership award or just an experiment. Asking questions becomes imperative, but asking premature questions will get you premature answers because a mentor has to get to know you first before they can tell your future. Here's an example of a premature question: "What career should I go into?" With this question, you can expect a premature/modest answer. Here's a better question: "I'm deciding between these two jobs, which each offer similar benefits and drawbacks. What do you think? Which factors should I consider most highly – salary, geography, etc.?" In this example, the mentee is providing options and opening up a conversation for an opinion. This is also a way to lead into a great discussion on career choices. Here's a common question mentees ask that I think is problematic: "What would you do if you were me /you were in my shoes?" This either means, "What would you do in this situation?" which is asking what the mentor would do after considering his/her own situation, which is not what you really want. Or, it means, "If you were me, you had all the same strengths, weaknesses, opportunities, and threats as me, what would you have done." Instead of leading

95

into a discussion like this, approach it with a scenario, especially if you are looking for an honest answer. No question is wrong, but when getting to know a mentor and allowing that mentor to get to know you, ask questions that lead to dialogue, the mentor is not the "Know it all," mentors also expect to learn from their mentees.

2) **Have strong beliefs, but be open-minded.** This is maybe the hardest model to consider: Mentors want to mentor someone they can influence in a positive way. Every mentor knows that success is the goal for every mentee, no mentor goes into a mentee relationship and believes that mentee is going to fail at everything or become a failure. Asking a million questions but putting forth no ideas of your own, or simply nodding at anything and everything the mentor says doesn't show initiative and really doesn't help with the process. By the same token, acting like you've figured out the world is just as much harder to build — who wants to help someone who thinks he doesn't need help? So how do you walk the line between these two extremes? Try articulating your current stance to your mentor in an expository fashion: here is what I feel,

here is why, here is my level of certainty, and here's how I think you can help. Being open-minded is helpful because it shows that you are really open to having a mentor and that you are willing to participate in the building process.

3) **Have a long term perspective.** Mentoring relationships are like any friendship or romance — it takes time. Lots of time. Years of time. If things are going well from the initial meet and greet, don't try to cover every topic on your mind in this one meeting. Dive deep. Have a memorable conversation about just a couple of things. Don't bring everything all at once, remember your goal is also evaluating the mentor. The same way you have to prove to the mentor that you are committed is the same thing they have to prove to you. If your goal is for this relationship to last long-term, make sure you have a positive perspective and share this with your mentor so that you both can be on the same page.

4) **Be open to topics not on your short-term agenda.** During the match process, mentees have a reason for picking who they want as their mentor for one reason

or another. Say you're trying to start a business and you meet with a start-up expert and you ask her to be your mentor. You want to pick her brain about successful start-ups. One problem: It doesn't always happen right away because as a mentor their goal is to make you better and to get to know you all around. For example, if you're young, everyone is going to want to give you advice about colleges and career choices. Be open to hearing it. In the long term, you'll have plenty of time to cover the topic that made you interested in her in the first place.

5) **Follow up by showing interest in them (at least three times a month).** To form a long term relationship, you need to stay in touch. But what does "stay in touch mean?" A meeting a year? An email every month? Phone calls? It all depends on the situation. We are now in the days of social media – we don't even have to call people anymore, but we can still be engaged with their life through social media. Make sure that your mentor has social media, if not there are several forms of communication channels that you can learn to use. However, nothing beats an in-person interaction. So aim for those, but it can be

hard to schedule time especially if you have an active schedule, but the goal is to make time. If the mentor is making time for you, then you can come to an agreed date and time to see one another. Remember, in your communications, show interest in your mentor's life, and they'll reciprocate and show in your life. If the mentor reads blogs, maintaining a blog is one of the best ways to stay in touch. Find ways to interact and show interest with your mentor. Show that you can be the initiator and not always the receiver.

6) **Don't make the mentor do the work.** It's not up to the mentor to figure out how to mentor you. It's up to you to figure out what you need help on. Help the mentor out by being engaged and coming up with different ideas or things you would like to do or discuss. This relationship is a two-way street. The mentor will do his part, and you will have to do yours.

Now that you understand the highly effective models of becoming a mentee, think about how a house is built, you have the base, the actual structure and then the roof. Now compare the building of a house to the building of a mentee-mentor relationship. Foundation is the hardest part because you want to make sure that you will be building this relationship on a sturdy ground where the stability is strong and secure. To ensure that this part is established correctly, consider planning, reflecting, observing, communicating, and learning the tools you would need to build the proper foundation for your relationship.

BUILDING A FOUNDATION BEGINS WITH THE MENTEE

Planner: The planning foundation includes seeking out ways for the potential mentor to be effective. Here you would ask yourself what type of mentor do- I want. This question can get tricky because depending on the type of mentee you are, you could be one that is completely new to this language of mentor and mentee and not know where to begin or you could be one to respond right away. Build out a blueprint of what role model you want to emulate; you can start by listing a few of your favorite people that you admire and write next to their name, their skills, and accomplishments. When the list is completed, then insert another column and create a list of your skills, accomplishments, and future goals. Planning can begin with small objectives, but overall a mentee's plan should include his or her vision of the future and the steps needed to achieve it. One goal may be for a mentee who needs help with speaking in front of an audience and may want someone who is exceptional at doing this. The important part of planning and goal-setting is execution and this part comes from when you pick your mentor. Too often great goals go unachieved due to lack of planning and writing them down. As a mentee, you have the upper hand because the primary goal of a mentor is to make you successful and one way you can be made successful is by you achieving your most important goals (if not all). When you first meet your mentor, make sure that you pull out your list that you built so that your goals can be follow-through and not forgotten.

Reflector: When building the foundation of the house, you also want to reflect on the process not just when it's complete, this is the same for your mentor relationship. Reflecting on your why is important, why should I have a mentor? Reminding yourself about the value a mentor has or could have in your life. You can also jot down important topics that you would want to share with your mentor that you would like advice on. Reflecting can help develop self-awareness. What are my strengths? Weaknesses? What are my communication preferences and why?

Observer: A great deal of our learning comes from observation, so it's important to develop this skill. Many builders try not to rush through the foundation part so quickly, sometimes they stop and look before they continue, and they even call others to observe to make sure there are no cracks or missing holes that have not been filled. One way you can observe is through observing mentors in action which can be beneficial—learning both from their successes and their mistakes. Speaking to friends who have mentors or to adults who have mentors and why they choose to have a mentor. You can start with your teacher or principal at your school and ask them if they ever had a mentor. Maybe ask them follow-up questions that can help you determine if it's best for you to have one as well. Observation can also help to identify developmental opportunities and threats that you see in yourself or other relationships.

Communicator: This is the part where you ask questions before you seal the deal because after this, the foundation gets covered completely. Mentees must communicate their thoughts and feelings regularly and honestly. Listening to constructive feedback may be tough, but it's also essential. Mentees need to embrace their shortcomings and continue to work on them. The mentee also should explain her communication preferences at the onset of the relationship. Communicate your wants and desires and make sure the connection is there, do not just pick a mentor because they have on nice clothes, unless you are into fashion and design. Communicate things in common and differences, as well as future goals.

Learner: One goal with building a house is that you will want to build another one. So the most important thing is to learn, which means ask questions during the process. Mentees are, first and foremost, learners. Without a mentee's genuine desire to learn and improve, the mentoring relationship is ill-fated. Learning is fundamental, if you feel your mentor can not teach you anything, then you will have to ask them challenging questions. One thing is true; you can always learn something from someone.

Are You Ready to be a Mentee?

- I accept full responsibility for my career goals and would benefit from guidance in creating a plan for my development.

- I am prepared to listen, but I understand that I am also expected to contribute to the relationship by sharing my ideas.

- I will accept constructive feedback and take the risk of exploring new ideas and approaches suggested by my mentor.

- My expectations for my mentoring relationship are well-thought out and realistic.

CHAPTER 7: THE ASK

Often, it takes a great deal of courage to ask for an adult figure to be your mentor. Knowing how to seek out mentors requires determination and skill. "Good Morning Ms. Felicia, I'm very interested in joining your mentorship. I want you to be my mentor because you are a great role model, and I look up to you." Sincerely, an interested future mentee.

"I realized that searching for a mentor has become the professional equivalent of waiting for Prince Charming. We all grew up on the fairy tale "Sleeping Beauty," which instructs young women that if they just wait for their prince to arrive, they will be kissed and whisked away on a white horse to live happily ever after. Now, young women and men are told that if they can just find the right mentor, they will be pushed up the ladder and whisked away to the corner office to live happily ever after." Sheryl Sandberg crafted these exact words in her book *Lean In*.

Mentors do not just fall out of the sky, nor do they appear when our situations are doomed. Asking is the most important and one of the main ways to obtain a mentor whether it's formed through a formal encounter or an informal one. Mentoring is a professional activity, a trusted relationship, a meaningful commitment. You as a mentee have to show that you are committed and that as a mentee you will do your part in establishing a mentoring relationship. There are several ways you can engage a mentor and make "the ask," but we will only discuss two ways. One is through a formal organizational structure (a mentoring organization) which are often mandatory such as joining an organization that promotes mentoring. An informal relationship consists of asking your sister's best friend to mentor you or even asking a church member. Whether the relationship is deemed formal or informal, the goal of mentoring is to provide both professional and personal advice to the mentee. A simple ask is where you begin, sending an email is one way to approach *The Ask*, but not preferred. Another way is through a meeting or a lunch outing. The important thing to understand is that you have to ask to begin the process toward mentorship. When engaging in a formal mentorship experience, the ask may be a bit easier, but it's not omitted. Some organizations do Speed Mentor Matching (similar to speed dating) when the mentee paired to one potential mentor face to face, during which time both participants may discuss whatever they like in a 3-5 minute format. After the time ends, the mentee rank the potential mentor and then the mentors switch, and the mentee starts the discussion and relationship all over again until the session is concluded. After all participants went, the mentees and mentors share score, and the ones that showed the most interest would pursue the ask.

What to look for when asking?

1) Choosing the right person as a mentor is probably the biggest factor to whether they'll accept your request. Most people want mentors who exemplify their vision of success—business leaders, entrepreneurs, recognizable names—it's easy to want to have a famous businessperson, developer, or activist as your personal mentor. Odds are though, those people are already busy or unavailable, and while it never hurts to ask, the odds are heavily against you. Remember, your mentor doesn't have to be a household name to be a good one—anyone with experience you can learn from and wisdom would make a great mentor. (I am not suggesting that "Oprah Winfrey" cannot be your mentor, you can also have her as an imaginary mentor (someone you never met, but you admire the things that they've accomplished and can imitate some of their work habits).

2) When you're looking for someone to be your mentor, look for people who have the title, position, or experience you're trying to get. Don't set your sights too far off into the future. Think about your next few career goals and look for people who match, preferably people you know personally or could easily meet. If your company, school, or Saturday program has a mentorship program, start there. Participants are looking for people to mentor, so you'll have an easier time finding someone willing to take you under their wing. If not, ask a friend or family member to connect you with someone in their company who's willing to take on a mentee and has the position you're looking for.

3) When you do ask someone to be your mentor, keep in mind that you're asking them for a favor—one that will likely require a good bit of energy on their part. You're not paying them for their time, and they don't owe you anything. If they're part of a mentoring program or have been a mentor in the past, they likely know this already, but even so, approach the question with the appropriate care, empathy, and lack of self-entitlement. The fastest way to get the old "Sorry, I

don't have time right now" response is to demand your prospective mentor's time and attention overconfidently. More importantly than the Ask is the approach. Take this part seriously, based on the age, you probably would not be approaching a potential mentor alone, so make it more comfortable.

4) Make your case based on common experiences and interests. Remember, getting a mentor to work with you is less of a job interview and more of a friend request. If you feel like their angle is "well, what do I get out of this," you may want to back off, but do let them know that you feel like you may be able to learn from each other if they'll give you a chance. If you do have common interests or hobbies, play that up too.

5) Explain you're looking for advice and guidance, not a tutor. Your mentor shouldn't do your work for you, and they should know from the outset that you're looking to learn from their experience—not have them essentially be the parent you ask for help every time you're stuck with your homework.

6) If your question seems to make your prospective mentor uncomfortable, back off. Mentors, like references, should be 100% dedicated to the task of helping you out. If you get the vibe that they feel pressured or don't really want to be in the position you're putting them in, let them out—if you force them into it, you won't get the best possible experience anyway, and worse, you may be imposing.

7) Once you've landed a great mentor, do what it takes to keep that relationship strong. Not only do you have someone you can learn from, but you'll have someone valuable in your professional network who can help you when the chips are down, or who can offer a hand to you when you have something to offer. When they give you advice, make sure you take it, and when you're not sure what you should talk about, ask them what you should be asking them.

These suggestions work whether you're in a formal relationship or informal one, "the ask" is still needed. It may be a little easier when you're a part of an organization because "the ask" was given during the application and match making process, however, it is still needed to officially break the ice in the mentor-mentee relationship.

Questions and Scenario's

Scenario 1: *Wrong Mentor Match*

You and your mentor hit it off right away. You were excited about your match until you started calling your mentor and they were not available. You were excited she likes you so much, but are unsure if she is available for you. You don't want to hurt her feelings, but you are feeling uncomfortable and avoided due to the unresponsive incidents. What should you do?

What should you do?

_____

_____

_____

_____

_____

Scenario 2: *Uncomfortable Conversations*

Your mentor has been trying to enter new conversations as an effort to connect with you better. He starts to ask about your social life and whether or not you're engaged in sexual activity. You are not comfortable with where the conversation is headed, but you have already been in the mentorship relationship for over one year.

111

How would you respond and why?

_____

_____

_____

_____

_____

Scenario 3: *Difficult Conversations and Scheduling*

After applying to 20 schools for college, you start receiving letters in the mail. You received a rejection letter from your number 1 school choice and you feel like you failed yourself, your family, and your mentor. You tell someone, and the only person you feel comfortable telling first is your mentor, but you don't want to be judged? It's Friday night and you've never asked if you could call your mentor on the weekend.

What do you do?

_____

_____

_____

_____

Are you ready to become a mentee and why?

_____

_____

_____

_____

_____

What type of person do you ideally want as a mentor? Can you describe the professional and personal qualities of this person? Do you want someone with the same hobbies, racial background or the same career path?

_____

_____

_____

_____

_____

How do you know as an individual that you are in need of a mentor?

_____

_____

_____

_____

What is a mentee to you?

_____

_____

_____

_____

_____

I would love to read your responses! Feel free to submit your responses to *felicia.onestepcloser@gmail.com* so that I can give you a shout out.

CHAPTER 8: THE ADJUSTMENT PROCESS

"A mentor didn't change who I was,
they added to who I was".

Getting adjusted to your mentor as a mentee is mandatory, especially if you want the bond to last and the building process to be effective. The point of developing a mentoring relationship is to adjust and to change to become a better you. A mentor can teach you a vast amount of skills that you did not know, and vice versa. As a mentee, do not be hindered nor afraid to express your concerns and to share your insight and knowledge because a mentoring relationship is a partnership/teamwork, you, as the mentee, have a right to express yourself, which is a form of adjustment (the act of becoming use to a new situation and the way of doing something to achieve a desired fit). Adjustment only happens successfully through respectful communication. One example of making adjustments through effective communication is scheduling appropriate times to chat and meetup. As a mentee, understanding your mentor's schedule at work, school, and other professional activities are important. The best and preferred way to interact with your mentor is knowing their schedule to avoid having to leave a voicemail. Making the adjustment if you know your mentor works 9-5 pm and goes to the gym until 6:30 pm then to possibly chat would have to be around 8 pm on weekdays and more flexible on weekends, understanding that sometimes you would have to chat on weekends. This also goes for the mentor when it relates to your schedule as a mentee, you have to make sure schedules are set in place and adjustments are understood. It is imperative to make sure that you resolve differences appropriately, professionally, and respectfully because it could potentially hinder the relationship and feel as if the mentor is not making time, but in all cases she is.

Mentoring creates meaningful connections that can positively impact the lives of both mentor and mentee. Those who receive mentorship are more likely to see improved academic, social, and economic skills. Those who mentor are able to build important leadership and management skills, while giving back to their community. The mentor-mentee relationship enhances teamwork ability because it allows two people to come together and add value to something that was already created. The value could be from making effective decisions, working in groups and listening, delivering ideas and implementing them, setting goals and achieving them. There are 46 million young people, aged 8-18, living in America. 16 million of them are growing up without a mentor. That's one out of every three young people who, outside of their family at home, don't have a trusted adult who they believe they can turn to for advice and guidance. Of those young people, 9 million face a variety of day-to-day challenges that put them at-risk for falling off track. The result of having a mentor is that they take you as you are and speak life into your situation. They bring out the best in you by allowing you to confront your past (whether its academics, low self-esteem, low moral) and work toward the now (what can you start doing differently now), they remind you that they were in the same situation. They do not point fingers at you or tell you what to do, no they allow you to change you (through guidance and advice).

Adjusting does not only mean accepting a mentor, but enhancing your growth and preparing you in other ways to make you a better you. Adjusting can go as simply as strengthening your communication skills especially in difficult conversations such as, changing "You Statements" to "I Statements" (taking ownership for our own faults). Often, when someone has a problem with another person, they tell them so by using a "you-statement." For example, "You promised to call me when you got out of your meeting at work!" While that statement may be true, by phrasing it that way, the listener is likely to get hesitant, and begin to disagree contentiously. Their response may be, "I couldn't because you forgot to send the calendar invite or a reminder text!" As we convert back to the beginning of Part I, we discussed interpersonal communication (i.e. tone) and how it can come off differently and affect the overall conversation. Instead of following the blaming statement (You Statement), a more considerate way would be to adjust your conversation with a more neutral form called "I statement." This statement is considered an easier way to avoid contentious engagements with a mentor or any individual when confronted with an uncomfortable situation without accusing them of being the cause of the problem. For example, the mentee could say, "When you didn't call me after your meeting, I got worried I didn't know if you got into trouble, and I didn't want to make the decision to submit my personal statement without your guidance, I really like how we work together and the unfiltered feedback you provide." The mentor's response to this statement is likely to be more conciliatory. For example, he might respond, "Thank you for being concerned. I'm sorry. We can still discuss the paper now if you have time or later today. Next time I will try harder to fulfill my obligations and keep our appointments, however if you noticed I didn't call you, its ok to send me a reminder text, a lot of things could pile up at once and I can forgot." This is one way to solve the problem and it also retains the good working relationship between the mentor and mentee, and is more likely to generate more cooperative interactions in the future than the you- statement. The "I statement" approach is worth it and can lead to a more sustainable relationship.

In my own experience, initially it was difficult adjusting to certain feedback that my mentor gave me. There was one incident where I wanted some agreement and support on a decision that I made, that concerned how I operated my tutoring business with a particular client. My mentor at this time was a successful entrepreneur and operated an effective business in serving others for the last twenty years. When I had to make a decision, I felt comfortable in making one on my own, instead of asking for her advice. I had a new client that showed interest in my service and we scheduled a session and agreed on the time and amount. I shared with my mentor that the client came 25 minutes late and I charged him a late fee for my time and to show business etiquette. Instead of her agreeing with my business decision, she expressed frustration with the choice that I made and my lack of giving it proper thought due to the fact that it was a new client. Her comment,

"As your mentor, it isn't necessary to tell someone there is a late fee for a service that you offer and a business that you are continuing to grow, if they called in advance to tell you that they will be running late due to another scheduled engagement they forgot about." With this reply, I felt that I was reprimanded for a business that I run and a business decision that I made. After speaking with her in person to gain clarity, I felt better about accepting her critique and learned a valuable lesson—mentors are there for your well-being and to help you to understand when you make mistakes and find the lesson in them. The lesson that I learned was, don't always make a decision based on the first encounter, communication is valuable that time, and scheduling is important and can mess up other scheduled clients. To avoid being late to other clients, a late fee will be charged if lateness occurs without 12 hours of advance notice.

The adjustment process is a *Two-Way Street*. Mentees should be able to find their own voice and outlet while mentors glean fresh perceptive for their own endeavors. It's important that mentors foster an environment where mentees can speak freely while addressing any of their concerns or questions. Mentors that simply talk at their mentees will offer little value, which are less effective. As a mentee, your obligation is to ask questions and to seek for clarity to learn from others' experiences. Mentoring is sharing. It's vital that mentors feel comfortable sharing their career experiences and mentees feel that the advice is accepted. Every relationship will not be an easy adjustment, but neither does it have to be completely unbearable.

It always require an adjustment when the thought of learning from your mentee becomes a state of reality. With many new technological innovations, new dance moves, college, and career-ready standards, order and trend-setting changes, this is the time to sit back and learn from what your mentee has experienced and is knowledgeable about. When your mentee tells you that they would like to be a mentor to someone because of their own experience, it is a joy of switching roles and growing from a mentee to a mentor; however, this switch does not negate the relationship that the mentor and the mentee have; it now becomes a triangle. This is a powerful way to demonstrate your trust and confidence and to build the mentee's sense of acceptance, competence, and self-esteem. The best way to accomplish this is to help the mentee (boy or girl) find a volunteer program that matches with his or her interest and bring together young people of different ages. As it is happening in the workplace, younger workers are bringing in new skills that are useful to

121

an organization. The switching experience involves a mentor who switches from adviser to the one being advised.

The goal of mentoring is to inspire other people to become mentors. So if your mentee becomes a mentor, you have done your job successfully. Traditionally, mentoring has involved the most experienced professionals offering best-practice advice to their entry level counterparts (mentees). But today and similar in the workplace, some engage in reverse mentoring in which younger (not experienced/entry level) mentees teach new tools and provide information on process improvements to the more experienced mentors.

Switching roles does not end up with mentors accepting this change easily. Reverse mentors and their mentees (protégés) can run into a few stumbling blocks. A big challenge is persuading seasoned mentors to embrace the role reversal and start taking advice instead of always giving it. They need to let go of their leadership role and learn the art of "followership," The saying, "Do unto others what others have done unto you" is a practice what you teach type of movement. In order for the Mentor Proclamation that was set before us by former president of the United States Barack Obama; to be fully celebrated and the need for more mentees to be paired with effective mentors to decrease the number of youth without positive role models, is to become more familiar with switching roles and being ok to learn from the young.

Switching roles is significant because it fosters true leadership, and the challenge that many are experiencing today is a lack of authentic leadership and the ability to fully adjust. In the long and short, as a mentee, you will be a mentee forever, there will always be someone you look to for guidance and advice. You never stop growing as long as you keep looking for people to learn from.

CHAPTER 9: MENTEE MODELS TESTIMONIALS

We can all agree that reading something is less effective then hearing testimonials from actual Mentee Models. Here we have actual mentees who share about their experience of being a mentee and having a mentor. They share about the role that they performed to make the relationship an effective and memorable one and the value that it has on their family. Each mentee model experienced there mentorship relationship differently, which you will as well. No mentorship relationship will be the same, but here are three unique stories from mentee models about the attachment process and the effects that each encountered.

Jideka Francis-Mae Long

12th grade student at Eastern High School

Since I met my mentor, the experience has been a lot of rocky roads. We've been through a lot since I knew her.

We've cried and we had a chance to build. She was always available and she knows everything about me. I trust my mentor as a mentor, second mother, and a life coach. My mentor guided me through a lot of life lessons. I've learned to be responsible, caring, and progressing to my life goals by learning from her and watching and listening to everything she tells me. Watching me grow from a pre-teen at the age of eleven until now at the age of seventeen has been some changes. My mentor never demanded me to change, but communicated her feelings and concerns for my decisions. Once I became a teen, I started to be aware of my surroundings and had a need to change them and my environment. I was not always happy at home, but when my mentor came to spend time with me (that) made a difference. She did not just take me out of my environment, she experienced it with me by coming into my household and building a relationship with my grandmother, father, mother, and siblings. My mentor is the best mentor ever. The attachment process appealed to me more when she showed commitment and care for who I am and where I could go or become. We are in this for a lifetime.

Aaron M. Williams

High School Graduate of Lawrence Academy Boarding School; Incoming Freshman at University of Miami

My experience as a mentee has been an extremely awarding and giving opportunity for both my mentor and I. My mentor is a female and she not only listens to all of my problems, but is someone I can vent to, she helps me take my like to the next level. My mentor exposes me to learning opportunities to improve my grades and community service opportunities and I have been a big supporter of all of her business ventures. She has a busy schedule, but has always been there when I needed her ever since I was twelve. At the same token, I am able to give her my youth and provide my perspective to cater to a teenager's perspective as she tries to provide for and connect to others like me, this is an example of switching roles and making adjustments. My mentor was open to me showing her different trends that are appearing in the youth community, this made me feel comfortable in sharing my experiences and ideas to her. I would not be the person I am today without her being a direct blessing in my life. She is more than a mentor, she is an inspiration and gives me the drive to do more in my everyday life.

Fayvia Cromartie-White

Registered Nurse

My mentoring experience did not work out for me. I was introduced by my sister's best friend who had already succeeded in everything that I wanted to become. However, I was not in a mental state of mind to really rely or confide in a mentor. My mentor reached out when her scheduled allowed, but it was not a good time for me. My communication was not reliable at the time, my cell phone either wasn't working or I ran out of minutes and did not have a way to restore. Finally, when we first had our first outing, we bonded and I was really ready to connect, but when I reached out, she was not available and I had already felt like the whole world was against me and I was not getting enough attention, so I shielded away and never reconvened. The point of my testimonial is availability is important, but self-evaluation is top priority. I could not become attached to my mentor at the time because I was not ready to trust another human. I was not ready for change in my life nor was I ready to listen to instructions or advice from a mentor. My question to you, are you ready for a mentor?

PART III:

THE

MENTORSHIP

EXPERIENCE

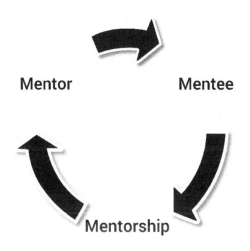

Mentor   Mentee

Mentorship

"Nobody, but nobody, can make it out here alone."

~ **Maya Angelou**

CHAPTER 10: THE MENTOR CODE OF ETHICS

There is a thin line between a mentor and mentee experience and that is the safety of the relationship. This can break the relationship as fast as your heart beats. Even if the mentee and the mentor are a perfect match, safety is the only means to a successful relationship. Every parents wants to know, "Will my child be kept safe?" This is stipulated in a formal binding mentor contract under any organization. Once a mentor signs a contract, they are agreeing that safety is a mandated necessity before they can release the mentee into their care. Every mentoring organization has a mentor undergo a background check, which includes finger prints, a list of references, and an application that asks for residency history and much more. In order for successful mentoring relationships to last, ethical guidelines have been created to protect both the mentor and the mentee from allowing uncomfortable and problematic situations to jeopardize the relationship. Drs. Jean Rhodes, Belle Liang, and Renee Spencer created and established the "Code of Ethical Principles" for mentoring. These women are pioneers in the research field of mentoring, where they focus the vast majority of their research in addressing ethics, social justice, and social change in the context of successful and unsuccessful mentoring relationships and programs. They are all professors at different colleges and universities in Boston, Massachusetts. Just as ethical guidelines are crucial in other professions (doctors, lawyers, psychologists), they are equally fundamental to successful mentoring relationships.

1) **Promote the Welfare and Safety of the Mentee**

   i. Mentors should work to benefit their mentees. Although this may seem straightforward, there are often competing ideas about what might be good for the mentee – This is a reminder to build rapport with your mentee, parents, and guardians. A mentor also has the ethical obligation to do no harm. This encompasses the more extreme forms of harmful behavior, such as sexual harassment, abuse, and exploitation. Formal mentoring programs use background checks and screening procedures, such as SafetyNET, and the incidence of such occurrences is minimal. Nonetheless, if mentoring relationships are formed through informal associations, difficulties can and often do arise, when there is no record of that mentor in a system. Training and supervision can help mentors recognize the boundaries and limits of their expertise and seek assistance from program staff when needed. Parents can also set boundaries for the mentor and the mentee when it involves activities outside of the normal environment.

ii. **Misuse of Power:** Given the different roles and ages of the participants, a power differential is inherent in adult-youth mentoring relationships. The gulf can widen when there are also differences in class and racial backgrounds. Mentors may not even be aware of the social inequities driving these differentials or how these can play out in interpersonal relationships (Fisher, 1997). Mentors may unwittingly put forth beliefs or opinions that conflict with the experiences and values of their mentee, creating encounters where tension or discomfort arises for the mentee. It has been said that controversial conversations that should be dismissed are religious or political ones because they can cause persuasion or raise conflict. If the conversation of one of these topics appears, it's ok to have opinions and be strong in your stance on them, but we should not persuade another to agree.

iii. **Inappropriate Boundaries:** Physical contact: Mentors fill a niche that lies somewhere between professional and kinship and are thus afforded greater latitude in what constitutes appropriate boundaries. For example, although there is nothing inappropriate in a mentor holding hands with his 6-year-old mentee as they cross the street, other instances of physical contact or seemingly benign gestures or comments can be interpreted differently. It is best to err on the side of caution, as there are many ways to show care and closeness that do not involve physical contact or even benignly-crossed boundaries.

iv. **Multiple roles:** Mentors should avoid entering into a personal, professional, financial or other relationship with their mentees (and family members) if such a relationship might interfere with their objectivity or ability to work effectively as a mentor, or might harm or exploit the mentee. For example, although parents might naturally gravitate to their child's mentor when looking for a paid math tutor, the volunteer may better serve the parents by connecting them with other resources. Other potentially compromising situations include mentors offering medical or legal advice to their mentees based on their professional expertise (e.g., medical, legal, psychological) without the proper parental consent. A mentor must also of course have excellent reflective and engaged listening skills. He or she must be objective and have an understanding of the confidential nature of the relationship, so that a relationship based on mutual respect and trust can be created and maintained.

2) **Act with Integrity:** This related principle highlights the obligation of mentors to be thoughtful and forthright about the commitments (i.e., time, financial) to the relationship and to avoid setting up false expectations. Mentors should be reminded about the importance of their obligations to their mentees, as well as the meaning that is placed on plans and events such that even minor disappointments and tardiness can accumulate in ways that erode trust and closeness. Mentors are expected to bear the greater responsibility for finding ways to effectively and consistently communicate with their mentees, to honor plans and commitments and to seek guidance and consultation from mentoring program staff or other professional sources should they find that they are unable to do so. Mentors also should conduct

themselves with integrity in their mentees' schools, homes, and communities by being respectful of customs and regularities and by not acting in ways that leave parents unsatisfied. Mentors need to keep as a reminder that the mentee is monitoring their every move, if we want our mentees to act with integrity, then we must create the road that they shall follow.

3) **Respect the Mentee's Rights and Dignity**: Except in extreme situations (e.g., abuse, neglect, and endangerment), mentors should seek to understand and respect the decisions and lifestyle of a mentee and his or her family. Respect for self-determination involves behaving in ways that enable rather than interfere with mentees' and their families' ability to exercise their own reasoning and judgment. Mentors should seek to understand the mentee's personal goals, desires, and values and not undermine the mentee's capacity to make his or her own decisions. Issues of confidentiality, which abound in mentoring relationships, have been given insufficient attention. Mentee's and parents often disclose deeply personal information to mentors, sometimes with specific injunctions against sharing it with the other. And, having a place to share private thoughts and feelings is an

aspect of mentor relationships that youth have identified as being particularly meaningful to them. Mentors can serve as important sounding boards for their mentee, particularly in adolescence when youth are exploring their identities and may experience new forms of conflicts in their relationships with their parents.

Should We Travel?

Mentoring can be immensely rewarding for both mentor and mentee, providing many opportunities to learn from and share with each other, gain new insights, and discuss experiences that enrich each person's perspective moving forward. Traveling is one form where both can experience a new reaction, but it requires the mentor to keep safety top of mind with your mentee. As a mentor, you have to make sure that the parent is aware of the location and time of your arrival, the time of your departure and expected time of arrival home. Additionally, the mentee should be aware of their surroundings and the different ports of transportation as well and ensure they know the nearest police station. Traveling is encouraged because you want to expose your mentee to as much as possible. Traveling can simply be to the nearest amusement park, anywhere outside of the mentee's home or school environment is a form of traveling. The actual goal during the mentoring process is to expose your mentee to new surroundings, new environments that the mentee has not seen before or has not been able to fully enjoy. Traveling builds conversation outside of their confront zone because now the mentee is in a space that they feel that they can trust you and now they are more likely to open up and tell you more about their lives. Remember, the goal is not to get into their business, but to build the relationship, so traveling is encouraged.

The most important thing to remember is that time spent doing things builds trust and a long-term relationship. In *100 Ideas to Use When Mentoring Youth* by Dr. Linda Phillips-Jones, Jean Ann Walth, and Carlo Walth, one mentor stated, "The best way for me to get to know my mentees is to find out something they're interested in and discover ways to enhance that interest." There are tons of interesting things that you as a mentor can do to expose your mentee to outside of their environment. Some of the ideas that Phillips-Jones compiled, based on research and observation from the field, of possible activities to do with your mentee are the following:

o Expose your mentees to try something new—food, a sport, or hobby in another city.

o Double Lunch: link up with another mentor-mentee pair for lunch.

o Go to a college fair together.

o Take a trip to an amusement park.

o Visit a college campus together. Take the official tour.

o Help them fill out job or college applications at a library downtown.

o Talk about money and budgeting, help them open up a bank account.

o Do volunteer work together. Sign up for National "Mentoring Day."

CHAPTER 11: THE RESULTS

Mentorship is now recognized as the most funded social investment that many foundations now make an effort to promote and advocate through their social responsibility as a part of their way of giving back. For example, The Clinton Foundation, 4 Sisters Organization, Obama Foundation, and more. This shows that the result is pivoting more than ever in the 21st century. Many celebrities have "hash-tagged" about the benefits more than ever before; this existence of mentorship goes way back and has a proven track record that cannot be changed or amended. Statistically on a national level, research demonstrates the benefits for students who are mentored is as follows:

- They are 52% less likely to skip a day of school than their peers.
- They are 37% less likely to skip a class than their peers.
- They are 46% less likely to start using illegal drugs than their peers.
- They are 27% less likely to start drinking than their peers.

- Finally, 76% of at-risk youth who are mentored have the desire to enroll in and complete college, in comparison with only 50% of non-mentored at-risk youth who have this desire.

The results is that we (USA as a whole) have a wide variety of mentoring programs such as, 100 Black Men, YWCA, Imentor, SisterMentors, Boys and Girls Club, Mentor, Big Brother, Big Sister, and more that are designed to meet the needs of young people and to recruit mentors. However, what you get on a local level is a never ending one. This world is ever changing based on the people that are impacted and poured into. Mentoring young people is a way to be great. It is a way to create miracles for our children and ourselves. Every boxing champion is a champion before they receive a heavy weight belt, they become a champion because of the people that call them champions because the work effort they put into becoming something greater and better for themselves, family and others to follow. The coaches that pour into these boxers are continuously giving tips, advice, and positioning them to move forward and to never give up. Mentoring is an infectious passion that is passed on with each encouraging word, supportive pat on the back, and proud smile. There will be times when a mentee feels that they failed or a time when a mentor feels that they failed a mentee by not having anything to give for a particular situation; that's ok, the beauty of this is that everyone gets knocked down. When fighters get knocked down, the coaches do not quit on them or give up and they don't tell the boxer that maybe they should try and pursue another talent. No, they continue to motivate them, share relatable stories with them about a time they got knocked down (whether it was physical or not), we need to encourage our mentees to get back up. The real result is that they have someone in their corner, whether a mentor is there in person or not, they remember the voice and the words that they shared when times get rough "to keep moving" or "I believe in you." We are all One Step Closer to something bigger and better, but no one can make it out here alone. Every successful person is successful because they had someone in their corner and that someone was a mentor. Mentoring is a life-affirming circle that has the power to heal the wounds and divisions of our society and that expands every time two people touch each other's lives as a mentor and mentee.

I asked a few mentees what the results of having a mentor meant to them:

- Someone that can vouch for you.
- Someone that becomes family.

- Someone that helps you achieve academically by raising grades.

- Someone who doesn't judge but understands.

- Someone who makes you understand your own mistakes.

- Someone who sends you motivational quotes that helps you through the most challenging days and situations.

The results of sustaining a mentoring relationship has to do with the cycle of mentorship, it's a renewable source that keeps being recycled. Once you become a mentor and attract a mentee and start the mentoring relationship, the result is that it is a never ending cycle. The result stems to recruiting other mentors and taking on more mentees to advise and guide, which keeps the cycle moving. Once you plant one tree and you see that the foundation is strong and the tree is blooming so well, you then become contagious and want to build more trees. The same is true for mentoring, the effect that it has is similar to the laws of attraction, once you say it and believe it, it then becomes emphatic and you start to see that mentoring then becomes a part of you. In addition, mentoring is an effective approach to build upon youth assets by increasing desirable behavior such as, academic performance, job performance, and reducing risk which includes, school dropout rate and substance use. Youth who are mentored are more likely to be enrolled in college and have a smaller likelihood of being depressed and a greater likelihood of being socially accepted, have a positive academic mindset, and have better grades. In return, mentors gain a youthful perspective from the mentees, which adds to their personal development and encompasses a chance to witness a shift in themselves by showing passion to others and the process if they were to do it all over again. They also feel a sense of purpose in themselves.

In fact, the hope is that more mentors who are patient, diligent, enthusiastic, and truly want to help others, are taking an oath to become mentors. I would not be the person I am today, albeit I am still maturing, if it were not for my mentors and the role I had for stepping up to become a mentor. The benefits of having someone that can lead you in your desired path with positivity and authenticity is an advantage. Even though I am writing this book to build more mentoring relationships, there is no real script, everything happens organically. Furthermore, with this read and others alike, you can become a little more prepared and position when you do go after your mentee and mentor.

Is it a Lifetime Thing?

Good mentoring relationships can conceivably last a lifetime, sometimes sparked by a single conversation. A sustained and supportive relationship with a caring mentor is the key developmental experience for a successful mentoring relationship. Remember, mentorship is not like a marriage or other permanent commitments where a legal document is attached; this relationship is bind by communication and trust. When a mentorship is associated within a program, the typical commitment maximum is two years. However, no one is obligated to build for two years and end the relationship. The timeframe in remaining an active mentor or mentee when it feels it should end, can become an uncomfortable position. One may feel that the relationship has come far enough to be independent. There is a minimum amount of time that a mentoring relationship must commit to in order to witness the impact and see the results is at least eight months, but there is no real maximum. There are many instances where mentoring relationships last a lifetime, where they never lose connection and may grow to becoming as close as family, this is based on the willingness of the two parties. However, there are times when a mentoring relationship can remain a relationship for a lifetime, but the communication can sometimes become infrequent once the mentee prepares for their transition phase, whether it's from high school to college or college to the workplace, this is when the communication can experience a lapse. One may ask whether this is a good time to end the relationship or remain active. Remember the goal and remember that a mentee is recommended to have various kinds of mentors for every aspect of their life. Depending on the stage that they happen to be in at the time determines whether the relationship should remain active, receive closure, or become lapse temporarily. If your mentoring experience started when the mentee was in elementary school and now they're off to college, there is a 70% chance that they will not need you as much, especially if they move away. This is an opportunity for the mentee to find another mentor who can help them access other opportunities and skills. This is also a great time for the mentor to encourage the mentee to get involved in mentoring programs and become a mentor and for you the mentor to acknowledge there mentoring abilities and boast about your mentee going off to college. Is mentoring a lifetime experience? Yes, because that relationship, whether the relationship ends in six months, twelve years, or sixty, will always be a part of the mentor and mentee's journey, particularly when someone inquiries about their success, they can attribute some of that success to their mentor.

This is not always true, but research has found that "All mentoring relationships come to an end," approximately one out of five mentoring relationships come to an early close, often within six (6) months, and only 45 percent last twelve months[13]. While ending a mentoring relationship can be hard for both the mentee and the mentor, with some forethought, mentoring relationships can end more smoothly. Mentors, mentees, and sometimes parents can feel sad, hurt, relieved, angry, happy or confused when the relationship comes to an end. Addressing closure early and throughout the relationship is one way to increase the chances that the closure process is healthy for the young person and the mentor. I like to always use this saying, "Sometimes you have to plant trees that you would not have the opportunity to sit under." This simply means, we cannot always build up and encourage our mentees and then reap the results, such as seeing them transition from high school to become the top CEO. We don't have to always expect closure periods, but they should not be remised. Closure can be difficult but it is a component of the mentoring relationship that one may have to face. However, closure can be a meaningful and mutually

---

[13] http://www.wakehealth.edu/JUMP/Terminating-the-Relationship.htm

satisfying exercise if both mentoring partners enter the discussion with a positive intent. It is often overlooked, especially if the mentoring pair may be meeting infrequently due to location distant or schedule; and therefore it conveys a natural inclination to let the relationship fade away, rather than having a formal discussion about ending the relationship. Regardless of whether the closure is planned or unplanned, steps can be taken to ensure that the process is as supportive as possible.

1) **Choosing a Date:** Once you've decided that the relationship has run its course, choose an end date and plan to meet with your mentor at least one last time. Tell your mentor that your next meeting will be your last so that he or she can prepare for it.

2) **Planning the conversation** (communicating honestly): Begin the conversation by thanking your mentor for his or her time and efforts. Talk about all the highlights of the mentorship, such as meeting or exceeding goals. Tell your mentor exactly why you are ending the relationship. For mentees who have accomplished their goals early, this will be an easy task. On the other hand, mentees who are ending their relationships because of a poor personality fit, lack of communication or other problems, might find it difficult to tell their mentors the

truth. Just because the mentorship didn't work out doesn't mean your mentor is "bad" or can't improve. Give honest feedback so that your mentor can be better in the future. Mention the advice that helped you the most, and diplomatically suggest areas where the mentor could have been more helpful. On the contrary, if one mentor did not work for you, don't give up on mentoring, find another one that is just more fitting. This just means to take more time in the building phase and ask lots of questions.

3) **Learning from the experience**: Take some time to reflect on what you gained from the mentorship experience even if the only thing you learned is what not to look for in a future mentor. In general, mentorships should last minimum of one year, so remember to set a target date when starting a new mentorship.

Reasons to End a Mentoring Relationship

A mentor-mentee relationship may end earlier than anticipated for a variety of reasons:

1) **Loss of interest:** The mentor and/or mentee may lose interest in participating in the program.

2) **Unfulfilled expectations:** If the mentee and/or mentor have expectations for the relationship that are not met, they are likely to feel dissatisfied and may end the relationship.

3) **Difficulty connecting:** Mentors and mentees may not be able to establish a close relationship. For instance, one or both may not have the skills to communicate effectively with the other person. It is also possible that mentors may not understand their mentee's cultural background, making it hard for the two to bond.

4) **Lack of support:** The mentor and/or mentee may not have the support they need from mentoring program staff or from the mentee's family to continue the relationship.

5) **Behavior issues:** The mentor or mentee may violate a program policy, refuse to cooperate with program staff or parents discipline regulations.

6) **Changing life circumstances:** The mentor or mentee may move, experience a personal crisis, or find that their schedule is too full to continue meeting.

7) **Opposites may not fit-** When having a male mentor and a female mentee, they may not relate to frustrations as much as a woman and vice versa. But don't object to opposite mentor-mentee relationships.

CHAPTER 12: MENTORING MODELS TESTIMONIALS

It is important that as a mentor you recognize that you and your mentee (the mentoring relationship) are a part of a wider circle of support. Every one of us needs mentoring relationships to form throughout our lives – guides to help us deal with the changes, challenges, and uncertainties that come at every stage of the journey. When you remember those who have mentored you, you want to pass it on. Here we have actual mentoring relationships, mentors and their mentees have shared their experience of being in a relationship and the results it brought for both partners. No mentorship relationship will be the same, but here are five unique stories about the results of committing to partake in the mentoring process and the effects that each encountered.

Krystal Leaphart and Chara Fennell

Special Asst. & Policy Associate for NOBEL Women, Community Leader, and Former Mentor for YWCA NCA.

I have been serving as a formal mentor for over 8 years. In that time I have also had the pleasure of being mentored by a number of different people as well. When I initially signed up to serve as a mentor, I didn't understand the impact of such a role. I knew that I wanted to work with high school-aged black girls and help them navigate life. Being that I was only a few years older than the group I wanted to work with, I felt that I wouldn't have to censor the conversations we could have as much as I would have for a younger group of girls. With this age group, I was able to listen and celebrate the diversity of their voices. In the beginning, I was shy with the girls. I couldn't figure out what exactly it was I could offer the girls, what they needed from me, and how I can connect the two. I found myself sitting back and listening and in hindsight that was the best thing I could have done. Since I was visible, but also managed to listen, was what most of the girls needed to build trust. After that, I found that it was easier for my mentee Chara and others to open up about what was going on in their homes, schools, and in their dating life. As time went on, I soon figured out that mentors can play different roles in their mentee's life. I have some girls that I work with that see my professional goals and want to do some of the things I've done. I also have mentees that are more like sisters. We group message all the time and hang out when we are able. I also have mentees that are a mix of the different roles. One piece of mentoring that is not as clear is the roles mentees would like you to play in their lives. It is important to ask them what they may have in mind for what the relationship can come to be. This is an exercise that I shared with one of my mentees Chara. From this interactive exercise, Chara informed me of three roles that mentees, for the most part, are not looking for in a mentor. One is a parent. As you and your mentee build your relationship, it may be tough trying to balance when to express yourself and when to be there for them to vent. Most mentees will ask you for advice if they believe they need it. It is also up to the mentor to judge the best time to share their opinion. The next one is a savior. As mentors, we should not feel pity for the situations some of our mentees may be in. We also cannot develop a successful relationship on the idea that you are in their lives to save them. When mentees are in difficult situations, sometimes being present is enough and makes the mentees feel safe. And the last one is, they are not looking for someone to break them down to be build them back up into what mentors think they should be. My best mentors are those that listen to me and help me down my own path, not the path that may have worked for them. I try my best to take that same approach with my mentees. Also, I had in mind that I would be constantly giving without receiving much from the relationship, which I didn't mind. Now, I like to believe that through this mentoring relationship, my mentees have changed my life more than I could've ever imagined. I now know how to successfully work in youth programming, communicate more effectively, and I have found my career path through working with black girls.

~~~~~~

Linnita Hosten and McKenzie Sherman

Author, Speaker & Inner Excellence Strategist.

I started mentoring unofficially in the fall of 2011. I realized that mentoring has forced me to create more relationships with community leaders, be more alert of opportunities concerning young people, and it has given me an outlet to transparently share my successes and failures with those closest around me. My sister McKenzie has been my ultimate protégé, she has allowed me to be the role model that does not try to act as woman without any scars and bruises, but she sees me striving to be better. This authentic relationship has stemmed from big and little sister to mentor–mentee. We still had to build the bond that enables trust for her to be open with her big sister due to the reason being we have the same parents. However, just by listening and being engaged has shaped our relationship even beyond my own understanding. Building with Mckenzie has also created a path for me to build with other youths and for her to seek other mentor role models. The dialogue and relationships I've engaged in over this topic from trainings, celebrations to recruiting has been rewarding. I am fortunate to see my sister and many mentees go off to college, excel in college, and prepare to enter the real-world. It is both fulfilling and uplifting to accompany others through their life journey.

Solomon Hill and Felicia Fort

Assistant Professor at Central State University

I am a product of many helping hands and as a result have become a change agent. As a service-orientated professional, it has been deeply rewarding seeing the impact I have had on so many lives as a mentor, role model, and friend. The greatest reward is seeing my protégés' transform their struggles into success. One being the author of this book, Ms. Felicia Fort, how she calls for guidance, updates me on successes and pitches ideas. Sometimes the beauty of our relationship is created when she just calls to ask for advice, but as I listen, she then finds the answers to her own dilemmas. Just knowing that you poured into someone by listening, being available, and maintaining self-control is remarkable. I am extremely proud of my mentees who have surpassed the glass ceiling, but also believed that upward mobility is not just the result of their own ability, but of people pulling others up and helping them out. As we climb, we shall never forget to pull others up, that is what mentoring is all about, because we once were looking up. As a member of Alpha Phi Alpha Fraternity, Inc. one of the lessons I endured during my life is to lift as I climb.

Twanisha Mitchell-Johnson & Mentor Models

Manager, Learning at ASAE: The Center for Association Leadership.

Mentoring has been such a rewarding experience for me. Many individuals focus solely on the time and energy it takes to mentor someone and don't realize how much of a reciprocal process it is in that it allows you to give to others while investing in your own personal and spiritual growth. When you invest in the life of a young person, you are also investing in your community and making a positive difference in the world. The road that I have been on, is connecting mentors and mentees together to form that long-term relationship that ultimately leads to success and the success of others. I have dedicated myself to mentoring and the mentoring philosophy because I know and have seen it work for myself and others. I am determined to continue to help and teach young people the values and beliefs that have served well in my life and the lives of so many mentoring relationships that I have been blessed to witness. For me, there are few things more gratifying than that.

~~~~~~

Elizabeth Strong and Youth Mentoring Program

Director of Straight UP, Community Leader, & Member of Delta Sigma Theta Sorority, Inc.

A mentor is a pleasure and a burden at the same time. I have had the opportunity to guide and help kids to be the great them. What a reward! At the same time, it is a burden because we know and see the powers that are working against them. What keeps me in the position to want to mentor is the love that is being displayed and the mindset—someone did it for me and it wouldn't be right if I didn't give it back. Knowing that I cannot change the environment of my mentees as fast as I would like to, helps me to continue to show up and care for them. With all the constraints and drawbacks that you see as a mentor during this mentoring relationship, you remember that mentoring comes from your heart. The reward will be the lifelong satisfaction of knowing that you've helped shape the course of a mentee's life by showing them the possibility and not the impossibilities.

CHAPTER 13: THE MENTOR BLOG

This chapter touches on the hidden topics that many do not touch on in the beginning of a mentoring relationship. These were questions posed on my blog about the mentoring experience and the behind the scene activities that are not always raised in the beginning such as clarifying, myths of mentoring, the difference between a mentor and a sponsor, how many mentees can a mentor have, and more.

OBSTACLES IN A MENTORING RELATIONSHIP

The Mentor:

During the course of a mentoring relationship, the mentor and mentee may experience "roadblocks." Roadblocks are obstacles that could hinder a developing relationship. There are obstacles unique to a mentor and obstacles that only a mentee may encounter. The following are obstacles that could confront a mentor:

1) A mentoring style that does not meet the mentee's needs or suit you: What happens when a highly organized mentor has a mentee with a relaxed work style? A creative mentee has a mentor who practices the "old school of thought?" An assertive mentor has a mentee with a reserved personality? Of course you can guess what would happen-frustration! As a mentor, your style of mentoring may not always match the needs of your mentee. Your mentoring style has a lot to do with who you are and how you work. If you are a detail-oriented person, you probably tend to give extensive directions or outline each step of an assignment. If you are a person who tends to see the "big picture," you probably are more inclined to give vague directions to your mentee. Of course, noting these differences does not make one style better than the other. However, differences in styles between you and your mentee can pose as an obstacle. Both of you need to understand each other's styles. Be flexible, but remember that disorganization and sloppiness warrant improvement rather than acceptance.

2) Frustration may also occur when you don't adapt your style to meet the developing needs of your mentee: As

your relationship evolves, your mentee's confidence grows as skills develop and successes are relished. You need to adjust your mentoring techniques to keep in sync with your mentee's evolution. In time, detailed directions or certain problem-solving strategies may be considered stifling by your developing mentee. Consider giving less and accepting more from your mentee. Once you evaluate your mentee and discover the required amount of guidance, you can determine what style is appropriate for your mentee.

3) Insufficient time: Another potential obstacle for mentors is insufficient time. Some mentors can't seem to devote enough time to their mentee. Other commitments in your schedule may prevent you from spending time with your mentee. If you start to sacrifice time with your mentee because of other commitments, he or she may lose faith in you and your mentoring relationship will suffer. Another obstacle involving time occurs when a mentor expects too much progress from the mentee, in an unrealistic amount of time. You need to give your mentee time to grow professionally and to make mistakes along the way. Try not to be impatient with your mentee and expect too much too soon.

The Mentee:

1) Peer jealousy: One problem for a mentee is the jealousy of peers who do not have a mentor. When others see a mentee getting key assignments and advancing rapidly, professional jealousy can occur. By the mentor showing a mentee how to act as an advisor, he or she can gain leadership experience and perhaps diffuse some of the jealousy. If this does not work, the mentor can advise the mentee to look at this as another opportunity for learning and to use his or her interpersonal skills to deal with the situation.

2) One party overstepping professional boundaries: Another problem that both the mentee and a mentor could face is when one party oversteps the professional boundaries of the relationship. This occurs when one party wants the relationship to become more "personal." This type of obstacle sometimes occurs in cross-gender mentoring relationships. The fact that mentoring involves a close and confidential relationship between an experienced and less experienced employee could result in this obstacle. This obstacle should not deter a cross-gender

mentoring relationship. It only means that people should be sensitive to the perceptions of each other.

3) An inappropriate attitude on the part of the mentee: Another possible obstacle involves a mentee's inappropriate attitude toward the mentoring relationship. Some mentees expect too much from their mentors - demanding more time and attention than they actually need. Others may expect to control their mentors. Be firm with your mentee about commitments and responsibilities. In terms of social etiquette, you must be supportive of your mentee and sensitive to cultural differences. For example, in some cultures, there is a preference towards modesty, reserve, and control. Whereas with another culture, directness or emotionally intense, dynamic, and demonstrative behavior is considered appropriate.

Mentorship Myths

Do mentors get paid?

Unlike coaches or consultants, mentors typically aren't paid. Mentors are in the community development business as a way of "giving back." It just feels good to share one's hard-earned knowledge with someone who is ready to learn and excel. But there's much more to it than that. Any relationship is more effective and rewarding when both parties benefit. You might be surprised to learn that being a mentor has many direct benefits — making connections, improving your skills, and increasing your knowledge. Mentoring is about Giving Back — but It Can Help You, Too! Multiple mentors are helping build a community where social innovators, social entrepreneurs, change-agents, and leaders at all levels can thrive.

What's the difference between a mentor and a coach — or consultant?

While there are many opinions about this, many believe there is a distinct difference. Mentors are more like smart friends — not someone who is selling anything. Mentors' first priority is to volunteer their time and share their knowledge, skills, and insights — their successes — and failures. Because the support is so personal, some mentoring relationships turn into lifelong friendships. There are many times when a coach or consultant can be very effective. You may connect with a coach's personal style or methodology and can afford to pay for their unique approach. Consultants or other experts (such as researchers or accountants) can provide specific expertise and do work on your behalf (such as draft a business plan or manage your social media).

How many people can one person mentor?

There is no rule as to how many one can mentor, as each mentor must decide how much time they can commit to mentoring. Because of the time and energy needed to mentor effectively, many suggest that the mentor develop one connection before deciding to take on another. But it's unlimited.

Is mentoring only for the youth and adolescents?

This is a typical question that many tend to ask. Mentoring does not have an age limit, you can be considered a mentor or mentee at any age. Many workplace environments have mentoring opportunities where the entry level employee will be mentored by the associate or the executive in the organization. Another is the CEO of a small organization might be mentored by a CEO or founder of a larger organization. There is no shape, size or age that can prevent anyone from being mentored.

Is it worth having a mentor or just a sponsor, is there a significant difference?

We are well aware of what a mentor is, but a sponsor is similar as in the process to building a sponsorship relationship still requires finding one, asking, and building trust. In a sponsorship relationship, doing is required before the sponsor can provide for you. One must show initiative and commitment, offer availability to assist the sponsor with support. The goal or the outcome of a sponsor is for someone to vouch on your behalf when it comes to employment, school acceptances, and awards. A sponsor can be anyone, but they are someone who is plugged into a great network of people. The same with seeking a mentor that is a great match for your choice of career or development, the same is true with a sponsor. You want to find a sponsor who is doing and achieving in a field that is of interest to you. Once you develop that sponsorship relationship, it becomes easy for that sponsor to vouch for you when it comes to employment openings, businesses, speaking opportunities, clientele development, and prestigious school acceptances.

Closing Paragraph

In Web Du Bois work, *The Souls of Black Folk,* he referenced, "Now is the accepted time, not tomorrow, not some more convenient season. It is today that our best work can be done and not some future day or future year. It is today that we fit ourselves for the greater usefulness of tomorrow. Today is the seed time, now are the hours of work, and tomorrow comes the harvest and the playtime." This is the charge that it is now that we accept our role whether as mentors or mentees, but in due time, today is the day not tomorrow.

DEDICATION TO MY MENTEE'S

It's time to deliver my purpose and reason... I overcome by the words of my testimony. This book is a testament of how God used me to help the lives of so many by becoming a mentor. It shows passion, commitment and the will power to continue and impact the lives of others. There are always times you want to give up, but God will show you why you're needed. Today my mentees are transitioning from 9th grade to 10th grade, 11th grade to 12th grade, 12th grade to college, from junior to college senior and a working professional. I am beyond grateful for the relationships I have grown to love and adore. The trust that has been built and the transferring of knowledge and motivation that has been shared. I am grateful for my mentees: Ashlee Robinson, Jideka Long, Aaron M. Williams, Moire Wright, Carson Wright, and Aye Diallo. I will continue to support, encourage, and be there for each of you. You each have grown to be awesome individuals and future designers, political leaders, authors, lawyers, artist, and professional athletes. I am proud to call you my life-long mentees. Continue the work.

FELICIA M. FORT

ABOUT THE AUTHOR

Felicia is a philanthropist, entrepreneur, and a mathematician (the best part is turning complex problems into simple ones), a dedicated leader, mentor to six youths and young adults, and mentee to several professionals. Felicia is a proud alumnus of Benedict College, where she earned her BS Degree in Mathematics. Felicia also received her MBA from Trinity Washington University. A proud member of Delta Sigma Theta Sorority, Incorporated. Felicia is the founder and visionary for One Step Closer Foundation Inc. a 501c(3) nonprofit organization creating employment and educational opportunities that will enhance individuals towards higher education, financial deferment, and professional development and become change agents in society. Services include tutoring in math and GED testing and other standardized assessments, plus school supplies and general homework assistance. Felicia runs a scholarship program through her organization called the Fort's Book Scholarship, which awards students every year by providing assistance to purchase their college textbooks. Felicia resides in Washington, DC and is the vice president of business operations for CNHED and an adjunct professor at her Alma Mata Trinity Washington University where she teaches Quantitative Methods (statistics), Introduction to Business and Information Literacy (research). Felicia lives by the following mantra, "The more you know about how to make your dreams real, the closer you are to fulfilling them. It's up to you to make it happen." She loves skydiving and daring herself to seek and live an adventurous lifestyle.

About the Book

It's a Call to Action. *The Mentor Model* is a book that speaks from personal experience, observations, and research about the importance of building and sustaining a mentor-mentee relationship. Research shows that every successful person has had the help of a mentor. The goal of this book is to inspire and persuade the reader (young and experienced professionals) to seek after mentees, and for aspiring professionals and adolescents to seek after a mentor. The mentoring relationship is a two-way street, as illustrated in this book. Mentoring can't wait. Former President Obama has issued a charge, asking everyone to join the movement that has helped so many people become successful. There are so many children, youth, and young professionals who wait in need of guidance and support to achieve their potential. Now is the time to accept the call to mentorship.

Made in the USA
Coppell, TX
12 May 2022